CONTENTS

Introducing the *TOEFL® ITP* Test

This Official Guide has been created to help you understand and prepare for the *TOEFL ITP* test. By preparing for the test, you will also be building the skills you need to succeed in an academic setting and achieve your English language learning goals.

TEST PURPOSE

The *TOEFL ITP* test is administered by your institution for a variety of purposes, including

- **Placement** in intensive English-language programs requiring academic English proficiency at a college or graduate level.

- **Progress monitoring** in English-language programs stressing academic English proficiency.

- **Exiting** English-language programs by demonstrating proficiency in English listening and reading.

- **Admissions to short-term, non-degree programs in English-speaking countries** where the sending and receiving institutions agree to use *TOEFL ITP* scores.

- **Admissions to undergraduate and graduate degree programs in non-English speaking countries** where English is not the dominant form of instruction.

- **Admissions and placement in collaborative international degree programs** where English-language training will be a feature of the program.

- **Scholarship programs**, as contributing documentation for academic English proficiency.

Your institution can choose when and where to administer the *TOEFL ITP* test. Many institutions also score the test on-site. Each section of the test is scored separately, and there is also a total score. Section scores will help you understand which specific skills need improvement and help you plan your further study of English. Your institution will determine minimum acceptable scores.

Your *TOEFL ITP* scores are valid for two years. However, scores are generally only valid at the institution where the test was administered.

TEST FORMAT

The test consists of three sections and takes about two hours.

Section	Number of Questions	Admin. Time	Score Scale
Listening Comprehension	50	35 minutes	31–68
Structure and Written Expression	40	25 minutes	31–68
Reading Comprehension	50	55 minutes	31–67
TOTAL	140	115 minutes	310–677

TEST CONTENT

The *TOEFL ITP* test has three sections: Listening Comprehension, Structure and Written Expression, and Reading Comprehension. All questions are multiple choice.

SECTION 1—LISTENING COMPREHENSION

The Listening section contains recorded material that includes the vocabulary, idiomatic expressions, and grammatical constructions typical of spoken English. The section tests comprehension of both short and long conversations and talks.

SECTION 2—STRUCTURE AND WRITTEN EXPRESSION

Section 2 consists of sentences that test knowledge of structural and grammatical elements of standard written English. These sentences include a variety of topics and give no advantage to students in specific fields of study. When topics have a national context, they may refer to United States or Canadian history, culture, art or literature. However, knowledge of these contexts is not needed to answer questions concerning the structural or grammatical points.

SECTION 3—READING COMPREHENSION

The Reading section contains reading passages and questions about the passages. After you read a passage, you will be asked about main ideas and important details. You will also be asked to make inferences based on given information, identify textual organization, figure out unfamiliar vocabulary based on context, and recognize referential relationships of pronouns and abstract nouns.

TEST TOPICS AND SETTINGS

The *TOEFL ITP* test uses topics and settings that you will find relevant in an academic environment—appropriate for both classrooms and campus life.

Academic Topics

Arts: fine arts, crafts, theater, dance, architecture, literature, music, film, photography

Humanities: history, political science, government, philosophy, law

Life sciences: biology, paleontology, biochemistry, animal behavior, ecology, anatomy, physiology, genetics, health science, agriculture, botany

Physical sciences: geology, astronomy, chemistry, Earth science, engineering, meteorology, energy, technology, oceanography, physics

Social sciences: anthropology, sociology, education, geography, archaeology, psychology, economics, business, management, marketing, communications

Campus-Life Topics

Classes: class schedules, class requirements, library procedures, assignments (papers, presentations, readings), professors, studying, field trips

Campus administration: registration, housing on and off campus, studying abroad, internships, university policies

Campus activities: clubs, committees, social events

General Topics

Business: management, offices, official documents, law

Environment: weather, nature, climate, environment

Food: types of food, restaurants, planning meals

Language and communication: mail, email, telephone use, messages, requests for information

Media: TV, newspapers, Internet

Objects: descriptions of objects, equipment

Personal: family members, friends, health, emotions, physical characteristics, daily routines

Planning and time management: future events, invitations, personal schedules

Purchases: clothing, shopping, banking, money

Recreation: sports, games, concerts, plays, art, books, photography, music, parties and gatherings, public lectures

Transportation: travel, driving, parking, public transportation, travel reservations

Workplace: applying for a job, on-campus employment, work schedules

HOW TO USE THIS BOOK/AUDIO PACKAGE

Use this package to familiarize yourself with the appearance, length, and format of the *TOEFL ITP* test. It provides you with instruction, practice, and basic strategies for increasing your English-language proficiency.

Chapter 1 provides an overview of the test, information about test scores, and general test-taking suggestions.

Chapters 2, 3, and 4 provide in-depth discussions of the kinds of questions that appear in each part of the test. Each chapter also includes practice questions and explanations of correct answers so that you will understand the skills that are being tested in each section.

Chapters 5 and 6 provide actual test questions to familiarize you with the test; Chapter 6 is a full-length authentic *TOEFL ITP* practice test that will give you an estimate of how you might perform on the actual test.

The CD-ROM packaged with this book provides the audio for the Listening Comprehension practice sets and test sections.

ABOUT *TOEFL ITP* TEST SCORES

Score Scales

The *TOEFL ITP* score report provides scores for each section of the test. There is also a total score.

Section	Score Scale
Listening Comprehension	31–68
Structure and Written Expression	31–68
Reading Comprehension	31–67
TOTAL	310–677

Score Reports

TOEFL ITP score reports provide valuable information to help you achieve your English language learning goals. Score reports include:

- three skill scores
- a total score

Additional information on your score report provides details about specific English language skills reflected by your scores. Your scores are also linked to performance levels of the Common European Framework of Reference (CEFR), an internationally recognized description of language ability. *TOEFL ITP* test scores are reported in relation to four CEFR levels:

- A2-elementary
- B1-intermediate
- B2-upper intermediate
- C1-advanced

It is the responsibility of your institution to give you your personal copy of your score report. You will receive your score report approximately seven days after answer sheets are submitted for scoring. Your scores are valid for two years.

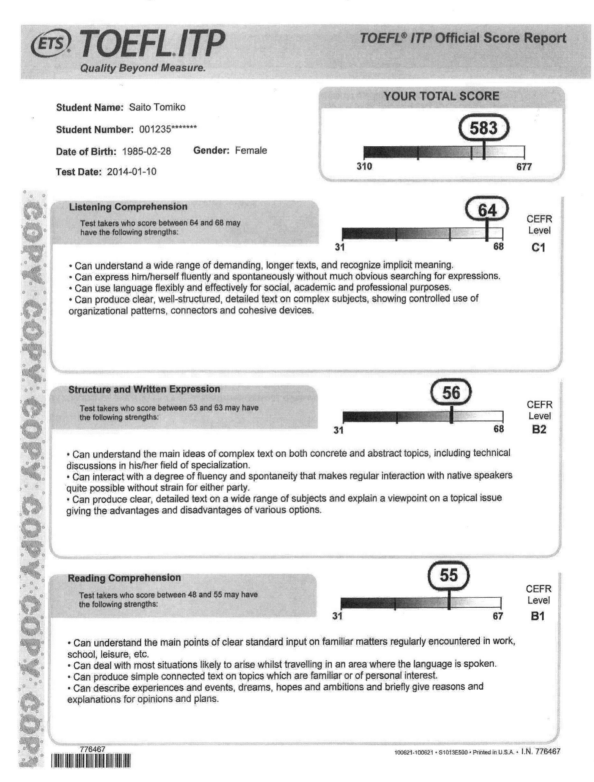

TOEFL.ITP
Quality Beyond Measure.

TOEFL® ITP Official Score Report

Student Name: Saito Tomiko

Student Number: 001235*******

Date of Birth: 1985-02-28   **Gender:** Female

Test Date: 2014-01-10

YOUR TOTAL SCORE

583

310   677

Listening Comprehension

Test takers who score between 64 and 68 may have the following strengths:

64

31   68

CEFR Level **C1**

- Can understand a wide range of demanding, longer texts, and recognize implicit meaning.
- Can express him/herself fluently and spontaneously without much obvious searching for expressions.
- Can use language flexibly and effectively for social, academic and professional purposes.
- Can produce clear, well-structured, detailed text on complex subjects, showing controlled use of organizational patterns, connectors and cohesive devices.

Structure and Written Expression

Test takers who score between 53 and 63 may have the following strengths:

56

31   68

CEFR Level **B2**

- Can understand the main ideas of complex text on both concrete and abstract topics, including technical discussions in his/her field of specialization.
- Can interact with a degree of fluency and spontaneity that makes regular interaction with native speakers quite possible without strain for either party.
- Can produce clear, detailed text on a wide range of subjects and explain a viewpoint on a topical issue giving the advantages and disadvantages of various options.

Reading Comprehension

Test takers who score between 48 and 55 may have the following strengths:

55

31   67

CEFR Level **B1**

- Can understand the main points of clear standard input on familiar matters regularly encountered in work, school, leisure, etc.
- Can deal with most situations likely to arise whilst travelling in an area where the language is spoken.
- Can produce simple connected text on topics which are familiar or of personal interest.
- Can describe experiences and events, dreams, hopes and ambitions and briefly give reasons and explanations for opinions and plans.

776467

100621-100621 • S1013E500 • Printed in U.S.A. • I.N. 776467

The *TOEFL® ITP* test measures the English proficiency of test takers whose native language is not English and assesses their ability to use the language in an academic setting.

TOEFL ITP scores can be used to make placement decisions, to monitor progress, and to inform end-of-course decisions. TOEFL ITP scores can also be used for admissions to programs and institutions where English is not the dominant language of instruction. Learn more at *www.ets.org/toefl_itp/use*.

The TOEFL ITP score report provides both section and total scores.

Sections	Scaled Scores
Listening Comprehension	31–68
Structure and Written Expression	31–68
Reading Comprehension	31–67
Total Score	310–677

The section scores are based on the number of correctly answered test questions, converted to a scaled score between 31 and 68 (or 67 for Reading Comprehension). The total score is calculated by adding the three section scaled scores, multiplying the sum by 10, and then dividing by 3. For example, if the scaled score for Listening Comprehension is 60, Structure and Written Expression is 60, and Reading Comprehension is 60, the total score is (60+60+60)*10/3 = 600.

To help you interpret the scores, a mapping of TOEFL ITP scores to the Common European Framework of Reference (CEFR) was conducted in 2011. Results of this study provide the minimum TOEFL ITP score for four of the levels defined in the CEFR (A2, B1, B2, C1).

In addition, The TOEFL ITP Program offers test takers the option to obtain certificates of achievement indicating the CEFR level that corresponds to their TOEFL ITP scores: a Gold certificate for scores at the C1 level, a Silver certificate for the B2 level, and a Bronze certificate for the B1 level.

TOEFL ITP scores are valid for two years. Because language proficiency may change in a relatively short period of time, scores that are more than two years old cannot be reported or verified.

Alternate Form

TOEFL ITP Examinee Score Report

Name: Saito Tomiko   Student Number: 001235

DOB: 02/28/1985   Sex: F   Degree: Times Taken TOEFL:

Native Country: Other
Native Language: Other

Purpose:

Scaled Scores: Listening Comprehension: 64   Test Date: 01/10/2014
                              Structure & Written Expression: 56
                              Reading Comprehension: 55
TOEFL.ITP   Total Score: 583
                                                                      Student's File Copy
                                                                      Do Not Copy

The *TOEFL* *ITP* Assessment Series is designed to be used for placement, progress monitoring, and exit purposes. *TOEFL* *ITP* scores can also be used for admissions to programs and institutions where English is not the dominant language of instruction for content courses. Learn more at **www.ets.org/toefl_itp/use.**

98151-16573 • FB413R200 • Printed in U.S.A.   I.N. 770462

CHAPTER 2

Listening Comprehension Section

The Listening Comprehension section is designed to measure your ability to understand spoken English in a variety of settings, both inside and outside of the classroom. These settings include lecture halls and classrooms, libraries, dormitories, offices, cafeterias, recreation facilities, and other public settings. Topics discussed are either academic topics or general topics that a university student might encounter at an English-language university, college, or institution. The section contains 50 questions divided into three parts and takes approximately 40 minutes to complete.

LISTENING TASKS IN ACADEMIC SETTINGS

Students in English-language universities, colleges, and institutions need English listening skills for understanding classroom lectures, of course. But students also need to interact with fellow students, administrative employees and professors in offices, libraries, cafeterias and recreation centers. The different types of listening tasks on the *TOEFL ITP* test reflect these various interactions and settings by including both academic and nonacademic topics.

In classroom and interpersonal interactions, it is necessary to understand the main topic being discussed as well as important details about that topic. But it is also important to recognize the purpose and attitude of other speakers and make inferences based on information you hear. The range of questions on the *TOEFL ITP* test reflects these different listening skills.

LISTENING TASKS ON THE *TOEFL ITP* TEST

The Listening Comprehension section is divided into three parts: short conversations, extended conversations, and short talks. Each conversation or talk is followed by one or more questions. You will hear the conversation or talk only once. You will then hear each question once and will have time to read and choose the correct answer from four written answer choices. The conversations, talks, and questions are not written anywhere for you to read; only the four answer choices are printed.

PART A: SHORT CONVERSATIONS

Part A consists of 30 short conversations. Each of these conversations consists of a two-line exchange between two speakers. The exchange is followed by a question about what was stated or implied by the speakers. The topics are typical of life on a university campus. For example, the speakers might talk about returning a book to a library, completing a homework assignment, or taking a bus. In addition, the speakers have many different purposes for talking to each other; for example, describing an event, offering advice, or extending an invitation.

Types of Questions in Part A

The questions following these conversations may ask you to identify the main topic or an important detail. You may also be asked to make an inference or a prediction based on what the speakers said. Other questions ask for the meaning of common idiomatic expressions or about the purpose of the exchange.

Type 1: Gist questions

Gist questions ask about the main idea of the conversation. The gist may or may not be clearly stated in the exchange.

Typical gist questions

- What does the man/woman mean?
- What does the woman/man say about X?

Type 2: Inference questions

Inference questions generally test information that is not explicitly stated in the dialogue. They often ask you to make connections between what the two speakers said.

Typical inference questions

- What does the woman/man imply?
- What does the man/woman imply about X?
- What can be inferred about the woman/man?

- What does the man/woman imply that X should do?
- What can be inferred from the conversation?
- What can be inferred about the speakers?

Type 3: Advice or Suggestion questions

Advice and suggestion questions ask what one of the speakers suggests or recommends that the other speaker do. The advice or suggestion may or may not be clearly stated in the dialogue.

Typical advice or suggestion questions

- What does the woman/man suggest the man/woman do?
- What advice does the woman/man give to the man/woman?

Type 4: Prediction questions

Prediction questions ask about what the speaker(s) will probably do next.

Typical prediction question

- What will the woman/man probably do (next)?

Type 5: Vocabulary questions

Vocabulary questions ask about the meaning of common idiomatic expressions.

Typical vocabulary question

- What does the man/woman mean?

PARTS B AND C: EXTENDED CONVERSATIONS AND SHORT TALKS

Part B consists of two extended conversations. The conversations usually take place in a university campus setting and cover a variety of topics common to the everyday life of university students. Examples of conversations include a student clarifying class information with a professor, a professor making recommendations about a student's assignment, or two students preparing an oral presentation.

Part C consists of three short talks. The talks have a single speaker, usually a university professor. The talks generally take place on campus, such as in a lecture hall or classroom, but they can occasionally take place off campus, such as in a museum or art gallery. The content is academic, and the topics span the arts, humanities, life sciences, physical sciences, and social sciences.

In Parts B and C, each conversation or talk is about two minutes long and is followed by three to five questions. The questions ask about information that was stated or implied by the speaker. Some questions ask about the topic or main idea, while others ask about important details in the conversation or talk. Some questions require you to make inferences about the speakers' purpose and roles.

Types of questions in Parts B and C

Type 1: Gist questions

Gist questions test your understanding of the main point or purpose of the conversation or talk. The gist may or may not be clearly stated in the conversation or talk.

Typical gist questions

- What are the speakers mainly discussing?
- What is the professor mainly discussing?
- What is the conversation/lecture mainly about?
- What is the purpose of the lecture/conversation?
- Why does the man/woman/student go to speak to the professor?

Type 2: Detail questions

Detail questions test your understanding of the important details in the talk or conversation. They can ask about what suggestions, advice, instructions, or warnings were given, or they may test your understanding of the meaning of key words or expressions. They may require you to connect two or more details in the talk or conversation or to make generalizations or inferences.

Typical detail questions

- Why does the professor mention X?
- According to the professor, what was the result of X?
- What does the student imply about X?
- What will the student/professor probably do (next)?

BASIC STRATEGIES FOR THE LISTENING SECTION

- In the short conversations, pay attention to the speakers' stress and intonation patterns. These will often give you information about the speakers' intended meaning.

- In the extended conversations, pay attention to the answers to questions asked by either of the speakers. These may include details that will be tested or indicate the importance of certain subject matter.

- In the extended conversations and mini-talks, pay attention to new words or concepts introduced by the professor. These will often be tested.

- Choose the best answer based on what is stated or implied by the speakers.

HOW TO IMPROVE YOUR LISTENING SKILLS

Listening is one of the most important skills necessary for success in both academic and nonacademic settings. The best way to improve your listening skills is to listen to different types of materials (such as lectures, discussions, and news reports) that cover a wide range of information.

Watching movies and television and listening to the radio provide excellent opportunities to build your listening skills. Audio recordings of lectures and presentations are equally useful. The Internet is a great source for listening material. Websites such as *www.npr.org*, *www.bbc.co.uk/radio*, or *www.bbc.co.uk/worldservice/learningenglish* are also excellent sources of material.

Here are some other ways you can strengthen your listening skills for the *TOEFL ITP* test.

Listening for Basic Understanding

- Increase vocabulary by listening to and reading English every day.

- Focus on the content and flow of spoken material. Do not be distracted by the speaker's style and delivery.

- Anticipate what a person is going to say as a way to stay focused.

- Stay active by asking yourself questions (for example, what is the main idea that the professor is communicating?).

- On sections of a piece of paper, make column headings labeled "Main Idea," "Major Points," and "Important Details." Listen carefully, and take notes while listening. Continue listening until all important points and details are written down, and then review them.

- Listen to a portion of a lecture or talk and create an outline of important points. Use the outline to write a brief summary. Gradually increase the amount of the presentation you use to write the summary.

Listening for Details

- Think about what each speaker hopes to accomplish. What is the purpose of the speech or conversation? Is the speaker apologizing, complaining, or making suggestions?

- Notice each speaker's style. Is the language formal or casual? Is the speaker's voice calm or emotional?

- What does the speaker's tone of voice tell you?

- Notice the speaker's degree of certainty. How sure is the speaker about the information? Does the speaker's tone of voice indicate something about his or her degree of certainty?

- Watch a recorded TV or movie comedy. Pay careful attention to the way stress and intonation patterns are used to convey meaning.

- When listening to a lecture, think about how the information is organized. Listen for signal words that indicate the introduction, major steps or ideas, examples, and the conclusion or summary. Words and phrases such as "first," "for instance," "next," and "finally" indicate the progression of ideas in a lecture.

- Identify the relationships between ideas. Possible relationships include cause/effect, compare/contrast, and steps in a process. Words and phrases such as "however," "on the other hand," and "in addition" indicate the relationship between concepts.

- Listen for words that show connections and relationships between ideas.

- Listen to recorded material. Stop the recording at various points and predict what information or idea will be expressed next.

- Create an outline of the information discussed, either while listening or after listening.

LISTENING COMPREHENSION PRACTICE SETS

In this section, you will become familiar with the types of questions asked in the Listening Comprehension section of the test. You will hear the directions, conversations, talks, and questions on the CD provided with this book. Only the answer choices for each question are printed. You should mark your answers on one of the answer sheets found in the book. At the end of each practice set you will find the answers and an explanation for each item.

PRACTICE SET 1—PART A: SHORT CONVERSATIONS

Now listen to Track 1 on the audio CD and read the directions below.

Directions: Now you will hear some short conversations between two people. After each conversation, you will hear a question about the conversation. The conversations and questions will not be repeated. After you hear a question, read the four possible answers in your test book and choose the best answer. Then, on your answer sheet, find the number of the question and fill in the space that corresponds to the letter of the answer you have chosen.

Here is an example.

On your recording, you hear:

Sample Answer
 B C D

In your test book, you read:
(A) He does not like the painting either.
(B) He does not know how to paint.
(C) He does not have any paintings.
(D) He does not know what to do.

You learn from the conversation that neither the man nor the woman likes the painting. The best answer to the question "What does the man mean?" is (A), "He does not like the painting either." Therefore, the correct choice is (A).

1. (A) A two-bedroom apartment may be too expensive.
   (B) The woman should not move off campus.
   (C) The woman should pay the rent by check.
   (D) The university has a list of rental properties.

2. (A) Talk to Dr. Boyd about an assignment
   (B) Return their books to the library
   (C) Meet Dr. Boyd at the library
   (D) Make an appointment with their teacher on Friday

3. (A) The transportation for the trip is free.
   (B) The class did not enjoy going on the field trip.
   (C) Some people may not go on the trip.
   (D) Everyone in the class has paid the fee.

4. (A) The woman should avoid getting cold.
   (B) It is easy to get sick in cold weather.
   (C) The woman should get more rest.
   (D) Dressing warmly can prevent illness.

5. (A) The woman should get another job.
   (B) He will not have to wait much longer.
   (C) The woman was mistaken.
   (D) He was waiting in the wrong place.

6. (A) He is probably nearby.
   (B) He should pick up his things.
   (C) He broke his racket.
   (D) He might be playing tennis right now.

7. (A) Watch the clock carefully during the final exam
   (B) Pick up their papers on the twelfth
   (C) Finish their assignment early
   (D) Discuss their topics after class

8. (A) She was not able to organize it.
   (B) Its location has been changed.
   (C) It has been rescheduled.
   (D) She does not know anything about it.

9. (A) The man is mistaken.
   (B) The error will be corrected.
   (C) She did not know about the problem.
   (D) Grades were sent late.

10. (A) Stay home and prepare for his exams
    (B) Attend the concert after his exams are over
    (C) Ask the woman to study with him
    (D) Go to the concert with the woman

PRACTICE SET 1—SCRIPT AND EXPLANATIONS

1. ***Woman:*** My lease is about to expire and I've decided to get a larger place. Do you know of any two-bedroom apartments for rent?
   Man: Have you checked the off-campus listings at the housing office?

   Narrator: What does the man imply?

   (D) This is an inference question. By asking "Have you checked . . . ," the man is implicitly suggesting that the woman should go to the housing office. Many universities in western countries have housing offices that offer students information about places to live.

2. ***Man:*** I've spent the whole morning at the library looking for the information we need—you know, for the assignment that's due Friday?
   Woman: I'm stuck, too. Maybe Dr. Boyd will have some suggestions.

   Narrator: What will the speakers probably do?

   (A) This is a prediction question. The speakers are looking for information they do not have. The woman proposes that the professor can help them.

3. ***Man:*** I think the whole class is going on the field trip next Friday.
   Woman: I'm not so sure. Not everyone has paid the transportation fee.

   Narrator: What does the woman imply?

   (C) This is an implication question. The woman implies that all students who were planning to go on the trip should have paid the transportation fee already. Since some students have not paid the fee, she does not think that the whole class will be going.

4. ***Woman:*** I can't seem to shake this cold.
   Man: Sometimes the only thing that helps is taking it easy.

   Narrator: What does the man mean?

   (C) This is a vocabulary question. The phrase "shake this cold" means to recover from a brief illness that involves sneezing and coughing. The man suggests that the woman "take it easy"; that is, get more rest.

5. ***Woman:*** Congratulations! I understand you got a job. When do you start work?
   Man: You must be thinking of someone else. I'm still waiting to hear.

   Narrator: What does the man mean?

   (C) This is a gist question. The woman thinks the man has a new job, but he replies that he is still waiting to find out if he was hired. He means that her statement is incorrect.

6. ***Man:*** Have you seen Jim around? We're supposed to play tennis.
   Woman: Well, his racket's here on the table.

   Narrator: What does the woman imply about Jim?

   (A) This is an inference question. The woman knows Jim's tennis racket is on the table, so she assumes that he is nearby.

7. **Woman:** I can't remember the due date for our final paper.

   Man: I think it's the twelfth, but the professor said not to wait until the last minute to hand it in.

   Narrator: What did the professor suggest the students do?

   (C) This is a suggestion question. The professor indicated that they should not wait until the due date to hand in the paper.

8. **Man:** Weren't you trying to get us all together for a picnic this weekend?

   Woman: It never really got off the ground.

   Narrator: What does the woman say about the picnic?

   (A) This is a vocabulary question. The idiom "to get (something) off the ground" means to get something started, so the woman is saying that she did not organize a picnic.

9. **Man:** I got my grades in the mail and there was a mistake in my mark for your course.

   Woman: I know—there was a problem with the computer system. It should be straightened out by next week.

   Narrator: What does the woman mean?

   (B) This is a vocabulary question. The woman says she is aware of the mistake in the man's grade and that it was caused by a computer problem. She uses the idiom "be straightened out," which means "be fixed" or "be corrected," to let the man know that the mistake will be corrected soon.

10. **Woman:** Can you come to the concert with me this weekend, or do you have to prepare for exams?

    Man: I still have a lot to do . . . but maybe a break would do me good.

    Narrator: What will the man probably do?

    (D) This is a prediction question. The man says it would be a good idea for him to take a break from his work, which suggests that he will go to the concert with the woman.

PRACTICE SET 2—PART B: EXTENDED CONVERSATIONS

Now listen to Track 2 on the audio CD and read the directions below.

Directions: Now you will hear a longer conversation. After the conversation, you will hear several questions. The conversation and questions will not be repeated.

After you hear a question, read the four possible answers in your test book and choose the best answer. Then, on your answer sheet, find the number of the question and fill in the space that corresponds to the letter of the answer you have chosen.

Remember, you are not allowed to take notes or write in your book.

1. (A) To get help in finding a new college
   (B) To change his major
   (C) To fill out an application for college
   (D) To find out how to change dormitories

2. (A) A small school does not offer a wide range of courses.
   (B) His tuition will not be refunded.
   (C) Changing majors involves a lot of paperwork.
   (D) He may not be able to transfer all his credits.

3. (A) He does not like his professors.
   (B) His classes are too difficult.
   (C) He cannot transfer his credits from his previous school.
   (D) He does not get along with his roommate.

4. (A) The registrar's office
   (B) The admissions office
   (C) The housing office
   (D) The math department

PRACTICE SET 2—SCRIPT AND EXPLANATIONS

Narrator: Listen to a conversation between a college student and his adviser.

Woman: Good morning, Steve. What can I do for you?

Man: Well, I've decided I want to transfer to a smaller college.

Woman: I know you've had a rough time adjusting, Steve, but I'm sorry to hear you want to leave.

Man: What I need to do now is find a new college and I was hoping you might have some ideas.

Woman: I might, but first I think I ought to warn you about some of the potential problems with transferring. The main one is how many of your credits will be accepted by your new college.

Man: You mean they won't all be transferable?

Woman: Not necessarily. It'll depend on what courses you've taken here and how they fit in with the requirements at the other school. So whatever college you choose, be sure to find out about transferring your credits.

Man: Who would I talk to about something like that?

Woman: First check with the admissions officer, then follow up with the registrar's office. Now . . . the other thing I wanted to caution you about is thinking that a transfer will solve all your problems.

Man: I'm not sure I understand what you mean.

Woman: Well, I know you haven't been happy this semester, but are you sure changing colleges is going to be the answer?

Man: Uhh . . . I like my classes, except for composition. The math department is everything I expected it to be, but . . . maybe if my roommate and I had hit it off better . . . that's really bothering me more than anything else.

Woman: Really? Did you talk to someone at the residence office? It might be that changing roommates would make all the difference.

Man: I might just do that!

1. *Narrator:* Why does Steve visit the adviser?

    (A) This is a gist question. At the beginning, the male speaker, a student, says "I've decided I want to transfer to a smaller college" to indicate his intention to transfer to a different college. Then, by saying "I was hoping you might have some ideas," he is asking for his adviser's help.

2. *Narrator*: What is one possible problem the counselor points out to Steve?

    (D) This is a detail question. The adviser says she wants to warn the man about potential problems and then points one out to the man—the risk that his credits might not transfer.

3. *Narrator*: What is Steve's main problem in adjusting to his college?

    (D) This is a detail question. In her role as adviser, the woman is trying to understand exactly why the man is unhappy. He says there are many things about the college that he likes, but the fact that he and his roommate have not become friends— they have not "hit it off"—bothers him most.

4. *Narrator:* Where will Steve probably go to get his problem solved?

    (C) This is a detail question requiring you to predict what the speaker will do next. In response to the adviser's question, "Did you talk to someone at the residence office?" the man says, "I might just do that!" It is likely that he will contact the housing office next.

PRACTICE SET 3—PART C: SHORT TALKS

Now listen to Track 3 on the audio CD and read the directions below.

Directions: Now you will hear a short talk. After the talk, you will hear some questions. The talk and the questions will not be repeated.

After you hear a question, read the four possible answers in your test book and choose the best answer. Then, on your answer sheet, find the number of the question and fill in the space that corresponds to the letter of the answer you have chosen.

Here is an example.

On the recording, you hear:

Now listen to a sample question.   **Sample Answer**
Ⓐ Ⓑ ● Ⓓ

In your test book, you read:
    (A) To demonstrate the latest use of computer graphics
    (B) To discuss the possibility of an economic depression
    (C) To explain the workings of the brain
    (D) To dramatize a famous mystery story

The best answer to the question "What is the main purpose of the program?" is (C), "To explain the workings of the brain." Therefore, the correct choice is (C).

Now listen to another sample question.   **Sample Answer**
Ⓐ Ⓑ Ⓒ ●

In your test book, you read:
    (A) It is required of all science majors.
    (B) It will never be shown again.
    (C) It can help viewers improve their memory skills.
    (D) It will help with course work.

The best answer to the question "Why does the speaker recommend watching the program?" is (D), "It will help with course work." Therefore, the correct choice is (D).

Remember, you are not allowed to take notes or write in your test book.

1. (A) The properties of quartz crystals
    (B) A method of identifying minerals
    (C) The life of Friedrich Mohs
    (D) A famous collection of minerals

2. (A) Its estimated value
    (B) Its crystalline structure
    (C) Its chemical composition
    (D) Its relative hardness

3. (A) Collect some minerals as homework
    (B) Identify the tools he is using
    (C) Apply the information given in the talk
    (D) Pass their papers to the front of the room

4. (A) When it is scratched in different directions
    (B) When greater pressure is applied
    (C) When its surface is scratched too frequently
    (D) When the tester uses the wrong tools

PRACTICE SET 3—SCRIPT AND EXPLANATIONS

Narrator: Listen to a lecture in an Earth science class.

Man: Today I'd like to explain the Mohs scale, used in what is called the "scratch test." This scale is based on the simple fact that harder minerals scratch softer ones. For example, a diamond scratches glass, but glass doesn't scratch a diamond; a quartz crystal can scratch a feldspar crystal, but not the other way around.

The scale is named for Friedrich Mohs, the mineralogist who devised it in 1812. His scale spans the range of minerals known at that time, from the softest to the hardest. By performing a scratch test using known minerals and a few common tools, an unidentified mineral sample can be placed between two points on the scale. By referring to the scale, the mineral can then be identified.

I have here a collection of the minerals included on the Mohs scale, as well as the tools necessary to complete this exercise. I'd like you each to take a mineral sample from the basket at the front of the room and classify it according to its place on the Mohs scale. First, however, I should give you a little warning. The hardness of any mineral depends on the strength of the bonds between ions or between atoms—the stronger the bond, the harder the mineral. Because bond strength may differ in various angles of a crystal, the hardness may vary slightly depending on the direction in which the mineral sample is scratched, so be sure to scratch each sample in several different directions.

1. *Narrator:* What is the lecture mainly about?

   (B) This is a gist question. While the main idea is often presented at the beginning of the lecture, sometimes you have to hear more of the lecture to completely understand the main idea. Here, from the initial part of the lecture, we know that the topic of this lecture is the Mohs scale, but we don't know what aspect of the Mohs scale will be discussed until the middle of the lecture.

2. *Narrator:* What aspect of a mineral is the Mohs scale used to identify?

   (D) This is a detail question. At the beginning of the lecture, the professor explains the basis of the Mohs scale—the relative hardness of minerals.

3. *Narrator:* What does the teacher ask the class to do?

   (C) This is a detail question. After explaining the Mohs scale in the first half of the lecture, the professor explains that he wants the class to try to classify minerals using the Mohs scale—to apply the information they've heard to a particular task.

4. *Narrator:* According to the teacher, when might the hardness of the same mineral seem to vary?

   (A) This is a detail question. At the end of the lecture, the professor explains why the hardness of a mineral might seem to vary if it is scratched in multiple directions.

CHAPTER 3

Structure and Written Expression Section

The Structure and Written Expression section is designed to measure your ability to recognize language that is appropriate for standard written English. It is intended as an indirect measure of your ability to write in an academic style rather than as a simple test of grammar. Nevertheless, to communicate clearly in academic writing, familiarity with correct grammar and word usage is essential. It is also important in listening and reading comprehension as well as speaking, especially in a university setting.

The Structure and Written Expression section contains 40 questions and takes 25 minutes to complete. There are two types of questions, with special directions for each type.

STRUCTURE QUESTIONS

Questions in the Structure part of this section are designed to test your ability to construct complete and grammatically correct sentences. In this section, you will be given sentences from a variety of academic or reference sources. Each sentence has a blank. The blank indicates where a part of the sentence is missing. You are also given four answer choices. Each choice consists of one or more words. You must identify the one choice that could be put into the blank to complete the sentence correctly.

Structure questions deal, in general, with the proper use of sentence elements to create complete sentences. The questions especially focus on larger units of syntax, such as clauses and phrases. Specific points tested include (but are not limited to) the correct formation and use of regular and irregular verbs; agreement between subjects and verbs; the correct formation and use of nouns, adjectives, and adverbs; comparisons; proper word order; and the appropriate use of pronouns, prepositions, articles, and conjunctions.

WRITTEN EXPRESSION QUESTIONS

Questions in the Written Expression part of this section are designed to test your ability to detect errors in academic writing. The questions consist of individual sentences adapted from academic or reference sources. Each sentence contains an error that might be made by a nonnative learner of English. Four parts of the sentence are underlined. You must choose the one part that must be changed to make the sentence correct in standard written English.

Some of the errors reflect grammatical problems related to agreement, parallel structure of words in a series, the formation or combination of words, or the use of articles, prepositions, and conjunctions. Others may involve the incorrect choice of a noun, pronoun, adjective, adverb, preposition, conjunction, or article. Sometimes a necessary word is missing or an extra word is wrongly inserted. Errors in word order might be included to test awareness, for example, that an adverb or adjective is out of place. Questions in the Structure and Written Expression section do **not** test your ability to recognize word-level punctuation errors, such as errors in the use of hyphens, apostrophes, or capitalization. These questions are also **not** designed to test knowledge of English spelling.

STRATEGIES FOR PREPARING FOR THE STRUCTURE AND WRITTEN EXPRESSION SECTION

The aspects of English that are tested in the Structure and Written Expression section must be understood within a larger context. This section tests the intermediate point between grammar knowledge and the skill of writing. Therefore, if you have the ability to write fluently and correctly in English, you will generally perform better on this section than if you simply memorize grammar rules but are unable to use those rules for communication.

In other words, knowledge of grammar rules does not, in itself, equal an ability to communicate in a language. Being able to recite a rule is not helpful if you are not able to make practical use of the rule. Rather, it is essential to be able to **use** grammatical rules accurately. Without accurate grammatical usage, meaning can be obscured or lost.

Therefore, to prepare for the Structure and Written Expression section, it is necessary to go beyond a mere understanding of grammar rules. In order to improve both your test scores and your skills in English, you should practice using these structures and rules in active communication.

In particular, to perform better on this section, you will need to use the grammar you have learned in a variety of writing activities involving communication. A variety of reading, speaking, and listening activities can also help you perform better. As you become increasingly proficient in communicating in English, your use of the grammatical structures that you have practiced will typically become more automatic, and your performance on this section will improve.

STRUCTURE AND WRITTEN EXPRESSION TIPS

Use English every day.

- Follow the tips provided in the Reading and Listening sections of this book.
- Set aside time each day to communicate only in English.
- Listen, read, and write in English every chance you get.

STRUCTURE AND WRITTEN EXPRESSION PRACTICE SETS

PRACTICE SET 1—STRUCTURE

This section is designed to measure your ability to recognize language that is appropriate for standard written English. There are two types of questions in this section, with special directions for each type.

Directions: Questions 1–10 are incomplete sentences. Beneath each sentence you will see four words or phrases, marked (A), (B), (C), and (D). Choose the one word or phrase that best completes the sentence. Then, on your answer sheet, find the number of the question and fill in the space that corresponds to the letter of the answer you have chosen.

Example I

Sample Answer

Geysers have often been compared to volcanoes ------- both emit hot liquids from below Earth's surface.

  (A) despite
  (B) because
  (C) in regard to
  (D) as a result of

The sentence should read: "Geysers have often been compared to volcanoes because both emit hot liquids from below Earth's surface." Therefore, you should choose (B).

Example II

Sample Answer

During the early period of ocean navigation, ------- any need for sophisticated instruments and techniques.

  (A) so that hardly
  (B) when there hardly was
  (C) hardly was
  (D) there was hardly

The sentence should read: "During the early period of ocean navigation, there was hardly any need for sophisticated instruments and techniques." Therefore, you should choose (D).

1. Telephone cables that use optical fibers can be ------- conventional cables, yet they typically carry much more information.

    (A) they are smaller and lighter
    (B) than the smaller and lighter
    (C) smaller and lighter than
    (D) so small and light that

2. In making cheese, -------, is coagulated by enzyme action, by lactic acid, or by both.

    (A) casein is the chief milk protein
    (B) casein, being that the chief milk protein
    (C) the chief milk protein is casein
    (D) casein, the chief milk protein

3. Sensory structures ------- from the heads of some invertebrates are called antennae.

    (A) are growing
    (B) they are growing
    (C) that grow
    (D) grow

4. An étude is a short musical composition written especially ------- a particular technique.

    (A) enable students practicing
    (B) enables students practicing
    (C) enable students to practice
    (D) to enable students to practice

5. ------- the United States consists of many different immigrant groups, many sociologists believe there is a distinct national character.

    (A) In spite of
    (B) Despite
    (C) Even though
    (D) Whether

6. ------- many food preservation methods for inhibiting the growth of bacteria.

    (A) The
    (B) Since
    (C) There are
    (D) Having

7. The safflower plant is grown chiefly for the oil ------- from its seeds.

    (A) obtained
    (B) is obtaining
    (C) which obtains it
    (D) obtaining that

8. Newspaper historians feel that Joseph Pulitzer exercised ------- on journalism in the United States during his lifetime.

    (A) influence remarkable
    (B) remarkable for his influence
    (C) influence was remarkable
    (D) remarkable influence

9. ------- must have water to lay and fertilize their eggs, while their offspring, tadpoles, need water for development and growth.

    (A) Though frogs and toads
    (B) Frogs and toads
    (C) That frogs and toads
    (D) If frogs and toads

10. The philosopher and educator John Dewey rejected -------.

    (A) to use authoritarian teaching methods
    (B) that authoritarian teaching methods
    (C) for authoritarian teaching methods
    (D) authoritarian teaching methods

PRACTICE SET 1—ANSWERS AND EXPLANATIONS

1. **(C)** In the main clause of this sentence, "telephone cables that use optical fibers" are compared to "conventional cables." Using the comparative form of the adjectives "small" and "light" followed by "than" correctly completes this sentence.

2. **(D)** A subject is needed to complete this sentence. In (D), "casein" is the subject of this sentence, even when followed by a noun phrase enclosed in commas that further identifies the subject.

3. **(C)** The relative (adjective) clause, "that grow from the heads of invertebrates" modifies the noun "structures." The other choices do not modify the noun correctly.

4. **(D)** The infinitive form of the verb is the only choice that completes this sentence grammatically. In this sentence, "to" of the infinitive is a shortened form of "in order to" and indicates purpose.

5. **(C)** Only the adverbial "even though" is a subordinating conjunction that can correctly complete the dependent clause of this sentence.

6. **(C)** This question tests the structure "there" + "be." The subject follows "be" when "there" is used. "There are" is required to complete this sentence correctly because the subject "methods" is plural.

7. **(A)** The passive form "obtained" is the only choice that completes this sentence grammatically. In this sentence, "obtained" is the shortened form of "that is obtained."

8. **(D)** An object is needed to complete this sentence. In (D), the noun "influence" is the object, modified by the adjective "remarkable," and these words are in the correct word order.

9. **(B)** A subject is needed to complete the main clause of this sentence. The subject here is composed of two nouns joined by "and."

10. **(D)** An object is required to complete this sentence. The noun phrase "authoritarian teaching methods" is the only choice that can act as the object of this sentence.

PRACTICE SET 2—WRITTEN EXPRESSION

Directions: In questions 6–10, each sentence has four underlined words or phrases. The four underlined parts of the sentence are marked (A), (B), (C), and (D). Choose the one underlined word or phrase that must be changed for the sentence to be correct. Then, on your answer sheet, find the number of the question and fill in the space that corresponds to the letter of the answer you have chosen.

Example I   **Sample Answer**

                                                        ● Ⓑ Ⓒ Ⓓ

Guppies are sometimes <u>call</u> rainbow <u>fish</u> <u>due to</u> the <u>bright</u> colors of the males.
                           A   B   C   D

The sentence should read: "Guppies are sometimes called rainbow fish due to the bright colors of the males." Therefore, you should choose (A).

Example II   **Sample Answer**

                                                        Ⓐ ● Ⓒ Ⓓ

<u>Serving</u> several <u>term</u> in the United States Congress, Shirley Chisholm became a <u>respected</u>
  A   B   C
United States <u>politician</u>.
                    D

The sentence should read: "Serving several terms in the United States Congress, Shirley Chisholm became a respected United States politician." Therefore, you should choose (B).

1. One of North America's <u>most</u> renowned <u>painters</u>, Grandma Moses was in her seventies
                                   A   B

    when <u>her</u> began to paint <u>seriously</u>.
          C   D

2. The novelty, relatively high speed, and <u>advantageously</u> of year-round service <u>made</u>
                                         A   B

    early <u>passenger trains</u> a popular <u>form</u> of transportation.
               C   D

3. <u>Because incomplete</u> records, the <u>number of enlistments</u> in the Confederate army
          A   B

    <u>has long been</u> <u>in dispute</u>.
       C   D

4. Estuaries are <u>highly</u> sensitive and ecologically <u>important</u> habitats, <u>providing</u> breeding
                  A   B   C

    and feeding grounds for <u>much</u> life-forms.
                          D

5. <u>When</u> the temperature drops <u>below</u> 68 degrees Fahrenheit, the body conserves <u>warm</u> by
     A   B   C

    <u>restricting</u> blood flowing to the skin.
        D

6. The Federal Theatre Project, the first federally <u>financed</u> theater project in the United
                                            A

    States, <u>was</u> established <u>to benefit</u> theater personnel <u>while</u> the Depression of the 1930s.
          B   C   D

7. Although best known <u>for great</u> novel *The Grapes of Wrath*, John Steinbeck <u>also</u>
                    A   B

    published essays, <u>plays</u>, stories, memoirs, and newspaper <u>articles</u>.
                  C   D

8. The political and <u>economic</u> life of the state of Rhode Island <u>was dominated</u> by the
                  A   B

    owners of textile mills <u>well</u> into the <u>twenty</u> century.
                       C   D

9. Lichens <u>grow</u> in a variety of places, <u>ranging</u> from dry <u>area</u> to moist rain forests, to
              A   B   C

    freshwater lakes, and even <u>to</u> bodies of salt water.
                         D

10. Musical instruments are <u>divided into</u> various types, depending <u>on whether</u> the vibration
                         A   B

    that produces <u>their sound</u> is made by striking, strumming, scraping, or <u>is blown</u>.
                C   D

PRACTICE SET 2—ANSWERS AND EXPLANATIONS

1. **(C)** "Her" is an object pronoun; the subject pronoun "she" is required here.

2. **(A)** "Advantageously" must be corrected to "advantage" to be parallel with the other nouns in the series.

3. **(A)** The preposition "because of" makes this sentence grammatical.

4. **(D)** The quantifier "many" must be used with the plural count noun "life-forms."

5. **(C)** The object of the main clause requires a noun phrase; the noun "warmth" is required here.

6. **(D)** The subordinating conjunction "while" is the wrong word choice; the preposition "during" is correct.

7. **(A)** A determiner must precede the noun "novel." Because the possessive pronoun "his" agrees with the subject of this sentence (John Steinbeck), the best determiner to use is the pronoun "his." The pronoun "his" must precede the adjective "great."

8. **(D)** "Twenty" is a noun; the adjective "twentieth" is required to modify "century" in this sentence.

9. **(C)** In this sentence, "area" must be corrected to "areas" so that it will agree with the plural nouns "places," "freshwater lakes," and "bodies of water."

10. **(D)** "Is blown" must be corrected to "blowing" to be parallel with the other "-ing" forms in the series.

CHAPTER 4

Reading Comprehension Section

The Reading Comprehension section is designed to measure your ability to understand short passages written in English. The passages are taken from college-level textbooks and books of general academic interest. Passage topics cover a variety of subjects at an introductory level; no specific background information is necessary to answer the questions, and there is no advantage given to specialists in particular fields of study. Sufficient information and context is provided in each passage so that you can answer the questions without having to rely on subject-specific knowledge outside the passage.

The Reading Comprehension section contains five passages, each 300–350 words long. There are usually nine to eleven questions per passage. You have 55 minutes to answer all of the questions.

READING TASKS IN ACADEMIC SETTINGS

Although a fair amount of information is communicated in classroom lectures and discussions, reading remains an important part of university education. To gain knowledge from the various texts assigned to you, you will need to consider more than the main idea and important details. Good readers also need to make inferences based on what they read, identify textual organization, understand unfamiliar vocabulary based on context, and identify relationships between pronouns and abstract nouns with concrete ideas stated in the text.

READING TASKS ON THE *TOEFL ITP* TEST

The Reading Comprehension section asks six different types of questions: Main Idea, Factual Information, Organization and Logic, Referential Relationships, Vocabulary in Context, and Inference.

TYPES OF QUESTIONS

Type 1: Main Idea

Main idea questions ask about the subject of the reading passage as a whole. They can also ask about the subject or main idea of one or more paragraphs in the passage.

Typical main idea questions

- What does the passage mainly discuss?
- The passage answers which of the following questions?
- What is the author's main point in the second paragraph?

Type 2: Factual Information

Factual information questions require you to identify central information and details explicitly given in the passage. They may also ask if information is true, not true, or not included in the passage.

Typical factual information questions

- The author mentions all of the following as a cause of X EXCEPT . . .
- Where in the passage does the author give an example of X?
- According to the passage, what is the least important aspect of X?
- According to the passage, which of the following is true of X?

Type 3: Organization and Logic

Organization and logic questions ask about the structure of a passage and its internal logic. You may be asked why an author mentions a particular piece of information, or you may need to identify the organizational structure of a passage.

Typical organization and logic questions

- The paragraph following the passage most likely discusses . . .
- In line *n*, the author mentions X because . . .
- The author mentions X as an example of . . .

Type 4: Referential Relationship

Referential relationship questions ask you to identify relationships between pronouns and other grammatical references to words or phrases used earlier in the passage. They ask for the noun or idea that is referred to later in the passage by pronouns or abstract nouns (for example, "this idea" or "this characteristic").

Typical referential relationship questions

- The word "these" in line *n* refers to . . .
- The "characteristic" mentioned by the author in line *n* most probably refers to . . .

Type 5: Vocabulary in Context

Vocabulary questions ask about the meaning of individual words and phrases as they are used in the context of the passage. They ask for a synonym or definition of an important word or phrase. Vocabulary questions may also ask for the literal equivalent of a word or phrase used figuratively in the passage. A vocabulary question may also be about a word that can have several meanings depending on the context.

Typical vocabulary questions

- The word X in line *n* is closest in meaning to . . .
- The word X in line *n* means that . . .
- The phrase Y in line *n* is closest in meaning to . . .
- In line *n*, the author refers to Y as X to indicate that . . .

Type 6: Inference

Inference questions ask for information that is strongly suggested in the passage. They have their basis in information that is explicitly given in the passage. For example, if an effect is cited in the passage, an inference question might ask for its cause. If a comparison is made, an inference question might ask for the basis of the comparison. From an explicit description of a new phenomenon, you could be asked to infer the characteristics of the old phenomenon.

Typical inference questions

- It can be inferred from the passage that . . .
- In the first paragraph, the author implies that . . .
- Which of the following can be inferred from the second paragraph about X?
- The author suggests . . .
- The passage supports which of the following conclusions?

STRATEGIES FOR INCREASING READING PROFICIENCY

As an English-language learner, you can improve your reading skills by reading extensively from multiple sources that cover a variety of types of writing and are written in an academic style (for example, business journals, science textbooks and nonfiction books). A wide variety of academic texts are available on the Internet as well as in magazines and newspapers.

READING FOR BASIC COMPREHENSION

- Develop the ability to skim quickly and identify major points.
  - o Practice skimming a passage quickly to get a general impression of the main idea instead of carefully reading each word and each sentence.
  - o After skimming a passage, read it again more carefully and write down the main idea, major points, and important facts.
- Choose some unfamiliar words in the passage and guess their meaning from the context (surrounding sentences); then, look them up to determine their meaning.
  - o Create flashcards to increase your vocabulary.
- Underline all pronouns (he, him, they, them) and identify the nouns to which they refer in the passage.
- Practice making inferences and drawing conclusions based on what is implied in the passage as a whole or in a particular paragraph.

READING COMPREHENSION PRACTICE SETS

PRACTICE SET DIRECTIONS

Directions: In the Reading Comprehension section, you will read several passages. Each one is followed by a number of questions about it. For questions 1–21, you are to choose the **one** best answer—(A), (B), (C), or (D)—to each question. Then, on your answer sheet, find the number of the question and fill in the space that corresponds to the letter of the answer you have chosen.

Answer all questions about the information in a passage on the basis of what is **stated** or **implied** in that passage.

Read the following passage:

The railroad was not the first institution to impose regularity on society or to draw attention to the importance of precise timekeeping. For as long as merchants have set out their wares at daybreak and communal festivities have been celebrated, *Line* people have been in rough agreement with their neighbors as to the time of day. The *(5)* value of this tradition is today more apparent than ever. Were it not for public acceptance of a single yardstick of time, social life would be unbearably chaotic; the massive daily transfers of goods, services, and information would proceed in fits and starts; the very fabric of modern society would begin to unravel.

Example I

What is the main idea of the passage?

    (A) In modern society we must make more time for our neighbors.

    (B) The traditions of society are timeless.

    (C) An accepted way of measuring time is essential for the smooth functioning of society.

    (D) Society judges people by the times at which they conduct certain activities.

The main idea of the passage is that societies need to agree about how time is to be measured in order to function smoothly. Therefore, you should choose (C).

Example II

In line 5, the phrase "this tradition" refers to

    (A) the practice of starting the business day at dawn

    (B) friendly relations between neighbors

    (C) the railroad's reliance on time schedules

    (D) people's agreement on the measurement of time

The phrase "this tradition" refers to the preceding clause, "people have been in rough agreement with their neighbors as to the time of day." Therefore, you should choose (D).

PRACTICE SET 1

Questions 1–11

As many as a thousand years ago in the Southwest, the Hopi and Zuni Indians of North America were building with adobe—sun-baked brick plastered with mud. Their homes looked remarkably like modern apartment houses. Some were four stories high and contained quarters
Line for perhaps a thousand people, along with storerooms for grain and other goods. These
(5) buildings were usually put up against cliffs, both to make construction easier and for defense against enemies. They were really villages in themselves, as later Spanish explorers must have realized, since they called them pueblos, which is Spanish for towns.

The people of the pueblos raised what are called the three sisters—corn, beans, and squash. They made excellent pottery and wove marvelous baskets, some so fine that they could
(10) hold water. The Southwest has always been a dry country where water is scarce. The Hopi and Zuni brought water from streams to their fields and gardens through irrigation ditches. Water was so important that it played a major role in their religion.

The way of life of less-settled groups was simpler. Small tribes such as the Shoshone and Ute wandered the dry and mountainous lands between the Rocky Mountains and the Pacific
(15) Ocean. They gathered seeds and hunted small animals such as rabbits and snakes. In the Far North the ancestors of today's Inuit hunted seals, walruses, and the great whales. They lived right on the frozen seas in shelters called igloos built of blocks of packed snow. When summer came, they fished for salmon and hunted the lordly caribou.

The Cheyenne, Pawnee, and Sioux tribes, known as the Plains Indians, lived on the
(20) grasslands between the Rocky Mountains and the Mississippi River. They hunted bison, commonly called the buffalo. Its meat was the chief food of these tribes, and its hide was used to make their clothing and the covering of their tents and tepees.

1   What does the passage mainly
    discuss?

    (A) The architecture of early
        American Indian buildings
    (B) The movement of American
        Indians across North America
    (C) Ceremonies and rituals of
        American Indians
    (D) The way of life of American
        Indian tribes in early North
        America

2. According to the passage, the Hopi
    and Zuni typically built their homes

    (A) in valleys
    (B) next to streams
    (C) on open plains
    (D) against cliffs

3. The word "They" in line 6 refers to

    (A) goods
    (B) buildings
    (C) cliffs
    (D) enemies

4. It can be inferred from the passage
    that the dwellings of the Hopi and
    Zuni were

    (A) very small
    (B) highly advanced
    (C) difficult to defend
    (D) quickly constructed

5. The author uses the phrase "the three
    sisters" in line 8 to refer to

    (A) Hopi women
    (B) family members
    (C) important crops
    (D) rain ceremonies

6. The word "scarce" in line 10 is
    closest in meaning to

    (A) limited
    (B) hidden
    (C) pure
    (D) necessary

7. Which of the following is true of the
    Shoshone and Ute?

    (A) They were not as settled as the
        Hopi and Zuni.
    (B) They hunted caribou.
    (C) They built their homes with
        adobe.
    (D) They did not have many
        religious ceremonies.

8. According to the passage, which of
    the following groups lived in the
    grasslands?

    (A) The Shoshone and Ute
    (B) The Cheyenne and Sioux
    (C) The Hopi and Zuni
    (D) The Pawnee and Inuit

9. Which of the following animals was
    most important to the Plains Indians?

    (A) The salmon
    (B) The caribou
    (C) The seal
    (D) The bison

10. Which of the following is NOT
    mentioned by the author as a
    dwelling place of early North
    Americans?

    (A) Log cabins
    (B) Adobe houses
    (C) Tepees
    (D) Igloos

11. The author groups North American
    Indians according to their

    (A) names and geographical regions
    (B) arts and crafts
    (C) rituals and ceremonies
    (D) date of appearance on the
        continent

PRACTICE SET 1—ANSWERS AND EXPLANATIONS

1. **(D)** This is a main idea question. Although architecture, movement, ceremonies, and rituals are mentioned in the passage, (D) best summarizes the general topic of the entire passage.

2. **(D)** This is a factual information question. Lines 4–5 of the passage state that "These buildings were usually put up against cliffs."

3. **(B)** This is a referential relationship question. The pronoun "They" refers to buildings. Although the other choices are also plural nouns, "buildings" is the logical referent for "they."

4. **(B)** This is an inference question. Because the passage states that the buildings were "like modern apartment houses" and that "some were four stories high," it can be inferred that the dwellings were highly advanced.

5. **(C)** This is a referential relationship question. Corn, beans, and squash are important crops that are mentioned just after the phrase "the three sisters."

6. **(A)** This is a vocabulary question. Clues to the meaning of this word are in the phrases "dry country" (line 10) and "brought water . . . through irrigation ditches" (line 11).

7. **(A)** This is a factual information question. The first paragraph suggests that the Hopi and Zuni lived in permanent homes in villages. In lines 13–14, the Shoshone and Ute are described as less-settled groups.

8. **(B)** This is a factual information question. The information answering the question is stated in lines 19–20 of the passage.

9. **(D)** This is a factual information question. The passage states in lines 20–21 that the bison was the chief source of food, clothing, and tent covering. "Chief" means "most important" in this context.

10. **(A)** This is a factual information question. NOTE: By using the word "NOT," the question asks the reader to remember which of the choices were mentioned and to recognize which choice was not or to review the passage to be sure. The correct answer is the choice that is NOT mentioned—in this case, log cabins.

11. **(A)** This is an organization and logic question. The author organizes the information in the passage by the names of various groups and where they lived, but does not refer to any of the things mentioned in the other options.

Questions 12–21

If the salinity of ocean waters is analyzed, it is found to vary only slightly from place to place. Nevertheless, some of these small changes are important. There are three basic processes that cause a change in oceanic salinity. One of these is the subtraction of
Line water from the ocean by means of evaporation—conversion of liquid water to water vapor.
(5) In this manner, the salinity is increased, since the salts stay behind. If this is carried to the extreme, of course, white crystals of salt would be left behind.

The opposite of evaporation is precipitation, such as rain, by which water is added to the ocean. Here the ocean is being diluted so that the salinity is decreased. This may occur in areas of high rainfall or in coastal regions where rivers flow into the ocean. Thus,
(10) salinity may be increased by the subtraction of water by evaporation or decreased by the addition of freshwater by precipitation or runoff.

Normally, in tropical regions where the sun is very strong, the ocean salinity is somewhat higher than it is in other parts of the world where there is not as much evaporation. Similarly, in coastal regions where rivers dilute the sea, salinity is somewhat lower than in
(15) other oceanic areas.

A third process by which salinity may be altered is associated with the formation and melting of sea ice. When seawater is frozen, the dissolved materials are left behind. In this manner, seawater directly beneath freshly formed sea ice has a higher salinity than it did before the ice appeared. Of course, when this ice melts, it will tend to decrease the
(20) salinity of the surrounding water.

In the Weddell Sea, off Antarctica, the densest water in the oceans is formed as a result of this freezing process, which increases the salinity of cold water. This heavy water sinks and is found in the deeper portions of the oceans of the world.

12. What does the passage mainly discuss?

    (A) The elements of salt
    (B) The bodies of water of the world
    (C) The many forms of ocean life
    (D) The salinity of ocean water

13. The word "this" in line 5 refers to

    (A) ocean
    (B) evaporation
    (C) salinity
    (D) crystals

14. According to the passage, the ocean generally has more salt in

    (A) coastal areas
    (B) tropical areas
    (C) rainy areas
    (D) turbulent areas

15. All of the following are processes that decrease salinity EXCEPT

    (A) evaporation
    (B) precipitation
    (C) runoff
    (D) melting

16. Which of the following statements about the salinity of a body of water can best be inferred from the passage?

    (A) The temperature of the water is the most important factor.
    (B) The speed with which water moves is directly related to the amount of salt.
    (C) Ocean salinity has little effect on sea life.
    (D) Various factors combine to cause variations in the salt content of water.

17. The word "altered" in line 16 is closest in meaning to

    (A) determined
    (B) changed
    (C) accumulated
    (D) needed

18. The word "it" in line 19 refers to

    (A) sea ice
    (B) salinity
    (C) seawater
    (D) manner

19. Why does the author mention the Weddell Sea?

    (A) To show that this body of water has salinity variations
    (B) To compare Antarctic waters with Arctic waters
    (C) To give an example of increased salinity due to freezing
    (D) To point out the location of deep waters

20. Which of the following is NOT a result of the formation of ocean ice?

    (A) The salt remains in the water.
    (B) The surrounding water sinks.
    (C) Water salinity decreases.
    (D) The water becomes denser.

21. What can be inferred about the water near the bottom of oceans?

    (A) It is relatively warm.
    (B) Its salinity is relatively high.
    (C) It does not move.
    (D) It evaporates quickly.

PRACTICE SET 2—ANSWERS AND EXPLANATIONS

12. **(D)** This is a main idea question. The passage discusses the processes by which ocean salinity is increased or decreased.

13. **(B)** This is a referential relationship question. The lines preceding line 5 talk about the process of evaporation; "this" refers to evaporation.

14. **(B)** This is a factual information question. The passage states in the third paragraph that ocean salinity is higher in tropical regions.

15. **(A)** This is a factual information question. Note that the presence of the word "EXCEPT" in the question means you must find the one answer that is not true. Evaporation increases rather than decreases salinity.

16. **(D)** This is an inference question. The other three options are not supported by the passage, but the passage does discuss a number of factors that affect ocean salinity.

17. **(B)** This is a vocabulary question. One can look at the discussion in the paragraph about increasing and decreasing salinity for clues to the meaning of "altered."

18. **(C)** This is a referential relationship question. In lines 18–19, the passage states that "seawater . . . has a higher salinity than it did before the ice appeared." "It" refers to seawater.

19. **(C)** This is an organization and logic question. The fourth paragraph talks about the formation of sea ice and the following paragraph, which mentions Weddell Sea, is there to give a concrete example of that formation.

20. **(C)** This is another factual information question. It is asking for the piece of information that is NOT true. Lines 17–19 state that seawater under ice has a higher salinity, so (C) cannot be true.

21. **(B)** This is an inference question. The final paragraph discusses seawater with a high salinity. The last sentence states that "This heavy water . . . is found in the deeper portions of the oceans of the world." This information supports (B).

CHAPTER 5

Sample Test Sections

In this chapter, you will find a full-length sample of each section of the *TOEFL ITP* test. This will give you a chance to practice the test section by section. After each section, there is an answer key and explanations for each question. The script for the Listening Comprehension section is also provided at the end of that section.

Each section of the test has a time limit. The recorded instructions will tell you when to start Section 1 and when to stop. You will need to use a watch or clock to time Sections 2 and 3. Remember that the time allotted for these sections includes time for reading the directions. If you finish Section 2 or 3 early, use the extra time to review your work.

Remember

- Work rapidly but carefully. Do not spend too much time on any one question.

- Some questions are harder than others, but try to answer every one. If you are not sure of the correct answer to a question, make the best guess you can and go on to the next question. It is to your advantage to answer every question, even if you have to guess.

- Mark your answer choices only on your answer sheet. During an actual *TOEFL ITP* test, you may not use notepaper, and you should **not** write or make any marks in the test book.

- Mark only one answer for each question. Fill in the space completely so that you cannot see the letter in the circle.

Use the answer sheet on the next page to record your answers for all three sections of the Sample Test.

SECTION 1

1 (A)(B)(C)(D)	21 (A)(B)(C)(D)	41 (A)(B)(C)(D)
2 (A)(B)(C)(D)	22 (A)(B)(C)(D)	42 (A)(B)(C)(D)
3 (A)(B)(C)(D)	23 (A)(B)(C)(D)	43 (A)(B)(C)(D)
4 (A)(B)(C)(D)	24 (A)(B)(C)(D)	44 (A)(B)(C)(D)
5 (A)(B)(C)(D)	25 (A)(B)(C)(D)	45 (A)(B)(C)(D)
6 (A)(B)(C)(D)	26 (A)(B)(C)(D)	46 (A)(B)(C)(D)
7 (A)(B)(C)(D)	27 (A)(B)(C)(D)	47 (A)(B)(C)(D)
8 (A)(B)(C)(D)	28 (A)(B)(C)(D)	48 (A)(B)(C)(D)
9 (A)(B)(C)(D)	29 (A)(B)(C)(D)	49 (A)(B)(C)(D)
10 (A)(B)(C)(D)	30 (A)(B)(C)(D)	50 (A)(B)(C)(D)
11 (A)(B)(C)(D)	31 (A)(B)(C)(D)	
12 (A)(B)(C)(D)	32 (A)(B)(C)(D)	
13 (A)(B)(C)(D)	33 (A)(B)(C)(D)	
14 (A)(B)(C)(D)	34 (A)(B)(C)(D)	
15 (A)(B)(C)(D)	35 (A)(B)(C)(D)	
16 (A)(B)(C)(D)	36 (A)(B)(C)(D)	
17 (A)(B)(C)(D)	37 (A)(B)(C)(D)	
18 (A)(B)(C)(D)	38 (A)(B)(C)(D)	
19 (A)(B)(C)(D)	39 (A)(B)(C)(D)	
20 (A)(B)(C)(D)	40 (A)(B)(C)(D)	

SECTION 2

1 (A)(B)(C)(D)	21 (A)(B)(C)(D)	
2 (A)(B)(C)(D)	22 (A)(B)(C)(D)	
3 (A)(B)(C)(D)	23 (A)(B)(C)(D)	
4 (A)(B)(C)(D)	24 (A)(B)(C)(D)	
5 (A)(B)(C)(D)	25 (A)(B)(C)(D)	
6 (A)(B)(C)(D)	26 (A)(B)(C)(D)	
7 (A)(B)(C)(D)	27 (A)(B)(C)(D)	
8 (A)(B)(C)(D)	28 (A)(B)(C)(D)	
9 (A)(B)(C)(D)	29 (A)(B)(C)(D)	
10 (A)(B)(C)(D)	30 (A)(B)(C)(D)	
11 (A)(B)(C)(D)	31 (A)(B)(C)(D)	
12 (A)(B)(C)(D)	32 (A)(B)(C)(D)	
13 (A)(B)(C)(D)	33 (A)(B)(C)(D)	
14 (A)(B)(C)(D)	34 (A)(B)(C)(D)	
15 (A)(B)(C)(D)	35 (A)(B)(C)(D)	
16 (A)(B)(C)(D)	36 (A)(B)(C)(D)	
17 (A)(B)(C)(D)	37 (A)(B)(C)(D)	
18 (A)(B)(C)(D)	38 (A)(B)(C)(D)	
19 (A)(B)(C)(D)	39 (A)(B)(C)(D)	
20 (A)(B)(C)(D)	40 (A)(B)(C)(D)	

SECTION 3

1 (A)(B)(C)(D)	21 (A)(B)(C)(D)	41 (A)(B)(C)(D)
2 (A)(B)(C)(D)	22 (A)(B)(C)(D)	42 (A)(B)(C)(D)
3 (A)(B)(C)(D)	23 (A)(B)(C)(D)	43 (A)(B)(C)(D)
4 (A)(B)(C)(D)	24 (A)(B)(C)(D)	44 (A)(B)(C)(D)
5 (A)(B)(C)(D)	25 (A)(B)(C)(D)	45 (A)(B)(C)(D)
6 (A)(B)(C)(D)	26 (A)(B)(C)(D)	46 (A)(B)(C)(D)
7 (A)(B)(C)(D)	27 (A)(B)(C)(D)	47 (A)(B)(C)(D)
8 (A)(B)(C)(D)	28 (A)(B)(C)(D)	48 (A)(B)(C)(D)
9 (A)(B)(C)(D)	29 (A)(B)(C)(D)	49 (A)(B)(C)(D)
10 (A)(B)(C)(D)	30 (A)(B)(C)(D)	50 (A)(B)(C)(D)
11 (A)(B)(C)(D)	31 (A)(B)(C)(D)	
12 (A)(B)(C)(D)	32 (A)(B)(C)(D)	
13 (A)(B)(C)(D)	33 (A)(B)(C)(D)	
14 (A)(B)(C)(D)	34 (A)(B)(C)(D)	
15 (A)(B)(C)(D)	35 (A)(B)(C)(D)	
16 (A)(B)(C)(D)	36 (A)(B)(C)(D)	
17 (A)(B)(C)(D)	37 (A)(B)(C)(D)	
18 (A)(B)(C)(D)	38 (A)(B)(C)(D)	
19 (A)(B)(C)(D)	39 (A)(B)(C)(D)	
20 (A)(B)(C)(D)	40 (A)(B)(C)(D)	

SECTION 1

1 (A)(B)(C)(D)	21 (A)(B)(C)(D)	41 (A)(B)(C)(D)
2 (A)(B)(C)(D)	22 (A)(B)(C)(D)	42 (A)(B)(C)(D)
3 (A)(B)(C)(D)	23 (A)(B)(C)(D)	43 (A)(B)(C)(D)
4 (A)(B)(C)(D)	24 (A)(B)(C)(D)	44 (A)(B)(C)(D)
5 (A)(B)(C)(D)	25 (A)(B)(C)(D)	45 (A)(B)(C)(D)
6 (A)(B)(C)(D)	26 (A)(B)(C)(D)	46 (A)(B)(C)(D)
7 (A)(B)(C)(D)	27 (A)(B)(C)(D)	47 (A)(B)(C)(D)
8 (A)(B)(C)(D)	28 (A)(B)(C)(D)	48 (A)(B)(C)(D)
9 (A)(B)(C)(D)	29 (A)(B)(C)(D)	49 (A)(B)(C)(D)
10 (A)(B)(C)(D)	30 (A)(B)(C)(D)	50 (A)(B)(C)(D)
11 (A)(B)(C)(D)	31 (A)(B)(C)(D)	
12 (A)(B)(C)(D)	32 (A)(B)(C)(D)	
13 (A)(B)(C)(D)	33 (A)(B)(C)(D)	
14 (A)(B)(C)(D)	34 (A)(B)(C)(D)	
15 (A)(B)(C)(D)	35 (A)(B)(C)(D)	
16 (A)(B)(C)(D)	36 (A)(B)(C)(D)	
17 (A)(B)(C)(D)	37 (A)(B)(C)(D)	
18 (A)(B)(C)(D)	38 (A)(B)(C)(D)	
19 (A)(B)(C)(D)	39 (A)(B)(C)(D)	
20 (A)(B)(C)(D)	40 (A)(B)(C)(D)	

SECTION 2

1 (A)(B)(C)(D)	21 (A)(B)(C)(D)	
2 (A)(B)(C)(D)	22 (A)(B)(C)(D)	
3 (A)(B)(C)(D)	23 (A)(B)(C)(D)	
4 (A)(B)(C)(D)	24 (A)(B)(C)(D)	
5 (A)(B)(C)(D)	25 (A)(B)(C)(D)	
6 (A)(B)(C)(D)	26 (A)(B)(C)(D)	
7 (A)(B)(C)(D)	27 (A)(B)(C)(D)	
8 (A)(B)(C)(D)	28 (A)(B)(C)(D)	
9 (A)(B)(C)(D)	29 (A)(B)(C)(D)	
10 (A)(B)(C)(D)	30 (A)(B)(C)(D)	
11 (A)(B)(C)(D)	31 (A)(B)(C)(D)	
12 (A)(B)(C)(D)	32 (A)(B)(C)(D)	
13 (A)(B)(C)(D)	33 (A)(B)(C)(D)	
14 (A)(B)(C)(D)	34 (A)(B)(C)(D)	
15 (A)(B)(C)(D)	35 (A)(B)(C)(D)	
16 (A)(B)(C)(D)	36 (A)(B)(C)(D)	
17 (A)(B)(C)(D)	37 (A)(B)(C)(D)	
18 (A)(B)(C)(D)	38 (A)(B)(C)(D)	
19 (A)(B)(C)(D)	39 (A)(B)(C)(D)	
20 (A)(B)(C)(D)	40 (A)(B)(C)(D)	

SECTION 3

1 (A)(B)(C)(D)	21 (A)(B)(C)(D)	41 (A)(B)(C)(D)
2 (A)(B)(C)(D)	22 (A)(B)(C)(D)	42 (A)(B)(C)(D)
3 (A)(B)(C)(D)	23 (A)(B)(C)(D)	43 (A)(B)(C)(D)
4 (A)(B)(C)(D)	24 (A)(B)(C)(D)	44 (A)(B)(C)(D)
5 (A)(B)(C)(D)	25 (A)(B)(C)(D)	45 (A)(B)(C)(D)
6 (A)(B)(C)(D)	26 (A)(B)(C)(D)	46 (A)(B)(C)(D)
7 (A)(B)(C)(D)	27 (A)(B)(C)(D)	47 (A)(B)(C)(D)
8 (A)(B)(C)(D)	28 (A)(B)(C)(D)	48 (A)(B)(C)(D)
9 (A)(B)(C)(D)	29 (A)(B)(C)(D)	49 (A)(B)(C)(D)
10 (A)(B)(C)(D)	30 (A)(B)(C)(D)	50 (A)(B)(C)(D)
11 (A)(B)(C)(D)	31 (A)(B)(C)(D)	
12 (A)(B)(C)(D)	32 (A)(B)(C)(D)	
13 (A)(B)(C)(D)	33 (A)(B)(C)(D)	
14 (A)(B)(C)(D)	34 (A)(B)(C)(D)	
15 (A)(B)(C)(D)	35 (A)(B)(C)(D)	
16 (A)(B)(C)(D)	36 (A)(B)(C)(D)	
17 (A)(B)(C)(D)	37 (A)(B)(C)(D)	
18 (A)(B)(C)(D)	38 (A)(B)(C)(D)	
19 (A)(B)(C)(D)	39 (A)(B)(C)(D)	
20 (A)(B)(C)(D)	40 (A)(B)(C)(D)	

Section 1

Listening Comprehension

Now set your audio player to Track 4.

In this section of the test, you will have an opportunity to demonstrate your ability to understand conversations and talks in English. There are three parts to this section with special directions for each part. Answer all the questions on the basis of what is stated or implied by the speakers in this test. Do not take notes or write in your test book at any time. Do not turn the pages until you are told to do so.

Part A

Directions: In Part A, you will hear short conversations between two people. After each conversation, you will hear a question about the conversation. The conversations and questions will not be repeated.

After you hear a question, read the four possible answers in your test book and choose the best answer. Then, on your answer sheet, find the number of the question and fill in the space that corresponds to the letter of the answer you have chosen.

Here is an example.

On your recording, you hear:

Sample Answer
● Ⓑ Ⓒ Ⓓ

In your test book, you read:

(A) He does not like the painting either.
(B) He does not know how to paint.
(C) He does not have any paintings.
(D) He does not know what to do.

You learn from the conversation that neither the man nor the woman likes the painting. The best answer to the question "What does the man mean?" is (A), "He does not like the painting either." Therefore, the correct choice is (A).

1. (A) He is majoring in economics.
    (B) He forgot to go to the bookstore.
    (C) He bought the wrong book.
    (D) He is selling his book to the woman.

2. (A) She appreciates the man's help.
    (B) Her presentation was somewhat long.
    (C) She needed more time to prepare.
    (D) She worked hard on her presentation.

3. (A) Search his closet
    (B) Buy a new wallet
    (C) Look in his coat pockets
    (D) Take off his coat

4. (A) He forgot about his appointment with the woman.
    (B) He did not finish his science project on time.
    (C) He cannot help the woman with her science project.
    (D) He will meet the woman at the library in 30 minutes.

5. (A) He has never been to a dormitory party before.
    (B) He does not like his dormitory room.
    (C) He agrees with the woman.
    (D) He finds the party much too noisy.

6. (A) She is happy she does not have so many exams.
    (B) She cannot help the man study.
    (C) She will not do as well on the test as the man.
    (D) The man should not complain.

7. (A) Karen is experienced at making salads.
    (B) It is easy to make a good salad.
    (C) The woman's salads are just as good as Karen's.
    (D) He is not sure why Karen's salads taste so good.

8. (A) Have the store deliver the couch
    (B) Try to get a discount on the couch
    (C) Delay the delivery of the couch
    (D) Rearrange the furniture in her apartment

9. (A) He thought the exhibit had closed.
    (B) He was confused about when the exhibit started.
    (C) He saw the exhibit last weekend.
    (D) He was not interested in meeting the photographer.

10. (A) Trying on clothes
    (B) Buying a mirror
    (C) Packing for a trip
    (D) Looking at travel books

Go on to the next page

11. (A) Make sure the cables are connected properly
    (B) Get a new printer
    (C) Replace the cables on the printer
    (D) Check the computer for lost files

12. (A) He does not know the way to the golf course.
    (B) He is probably not free in the afternoon.
    (C) He may not be a better golfer than the woman.
    (D) He is glad the woman has her own equipment.

13. (A) Wait for his headache to go away
    (B) Read a book instead
    (C) Take a different kind of medicine
    (D) Find out what the correct dosage is

14. (A) She did not plan to eat supper.
    (B) She is washing up for supper.
    (C) She did not want to come home.
    (D) She was planning to eat at home.

15. (A) The man plays the piano well.
    (B) The man should reconsider taking piano lessons.
    (C) She does not enjoy listening to music.
    (D) She does not have musical ability.

16. (A) He needed to call the bakery again.
    (B) The bakery was not open.
    (C) The bakery was sold out of bread.
    (D) The bakery does not make French bread.

17. (A) Go to the interview early
    (B) Do some exercise to relax
    (C) Tell the interviewer about his qualifications
    (D) Wear his new suit to the interview

18. (A) They do not know who painted the pictures.
    (B) They think modern paintings are creative.
    (C) They think children should be taught to paint.
    (D) They do not like the paintings.

19. (A) She will get a ride home with her parents.
    (B) She cannot go home until July.
    (C) She quit her job before summer vacation.
    (D) She is not going home for the summer.

20. (A) Jeff can give her directions to the rehearsal.
    (B) The woman should tell Jeff to come to the rehearsal.
    (C) Jeff might know when the rehearsal will end.
    (D) He does not know whether Jeff will be at the rehearsal.

Go on to the next page ➡

21. (A) He had to turn it off.
    (B) He could not hear it.
    (C) He enjoyed listening to it while
        working.
    (D) He was disturbed by it.

22. (A) Putting up posters now is a waste
        of time.
    (B) Most people have already voted.
    (C) The election results have already
        been posted.
    (D) Many voters are undecided.

23. (A) She has made a lot of progress.
    (B) She was always good in chemistry.
    (C) She travels a long distance to
        school.
    (D) She has been studying chemistry
        for hours.

24. (A) The man is a much better skier
        than he used to be.
    (B) The man lacks the ability needed
        to become a good skier.
    (C) The man should not compare his
        ability to hers.
    (D) The man should have taken skiing
        lessons as a child.

25. (A) His neighbors no longer grow
        peaches.
    (B) He keeps forgetting to ask his
        neighbors for peaches.
    (C) He is not sure what the woman is
        referring to.
    (D) His neighbors planted a new
        peach tree after the storm.

26. (A) He knows the manager of Jack's
        company.
    (B) He wants to help Jack move.
    (C) He is sorry he cannot help Jack
        manage his business.
    (D) He is doubtful that Jack's plans
        will succeed.

27. (A) Stay home and watch the news
    (B) Watch the program at a
        classmate's house
    (C) Tell Professor Jones the news
    (D) Meet Professor Jones at Dave's
        house

28. (A) Place an ad in the newspaper
    (B) Look in the student paper under
        apartments for rent
    (C) Check the notices posted on
        campus
    (D) Look at some apartments located
        near the student center

29. (A) He hopes the woman will not
        forget their lunch date.
    (B) There are some tennis courts
        available right now.
    (C) The tennis courts will be too wet
        to play on.
    (D) He wants to continue the game
        tomorrow.

30. (A) The man had already received the
        phone.
    (B) The phone will be installed soon.
    (C) The phone was already on order.
    (D) The phone had not been ordered.

Go on to the next page

Part B

Directions: In this part of the test, you will hear longer conversations. After each conversation, you will hear several questions. The conversations and questions will not be repeated.

After you hear a question, read the four possible answers in your test book and choose the best answer. Then, on your answer sheet, find the number of the question and fill in the space that corresponds to the letter of the answer you have chosen.

Remember, you are **not** allowed to take notes or write in your test book.

31. (A) A new book
    (B) An exhibit of photographs
    (C) A lecture series on transportation
    (D) Recent developments in urban transportation

32. (A) The editor of the school newspaper
    (B) The professor's student
    (C) The coauthor of the book
    (D) A subway company executive

33. (A) How it was financed
    (B) The engineering of the tunnels
    (C) Its representation in art and literature
    (D) Its effects on city life

34. (A) Show the reporter some photographs
    (B) Read an article in the campus newspaper
    (C) Explain how the subway tunnels were built
    (D) Examine a map of the New York subway system

35. (A) Setting up a computer class
    (B) Meeting a computer software vendor
    (C) Planning a computer fair
    (D) Arranging a trip to a computer company

36. (A) They attended a similar one the day before.
    (B) Too few members are interested in the activity.
    (C) The room is not available that evening.
    (D) The weather may be bad.

37. (A) At a computer software company
    (B) Far from the university
    (C) At the man's house
    (D) On the university campus

38. (A) The man will contact all the members.
    (B) A radio announcement will be made.
    (C) They will talk to the person in charge of publicity.
    (D) They will each call some of the members.

Go on to the next page

Part C

Directions: In this part of the test, you will hear several short talks. After each talk, you will hear some questions. The talks and the questions will not be repeated.

After you hear a question, read the four possible answers in your test book and choose the best answer. Then, on your answer sheet, find the number of the question and fill in the space that corresponds to the letter of the answer you have chosen.

Here is an example.

On your recording, you hear:

Sample Answer
Ⓐ Ⓑ ● Ⓓ

Now listen to a sample question.

In your test book, you read:

(A) To demonstrate the latest use of computer graphics
(B) To discuss the possibility of an economic depression
(C) To explain the workings of the brain
(D) To dramatize a famous mystery story

The best answer to the question "What is the main purpose of the program?" is (C), "To explain the workings of the brain." Therefore, the correct choice is (C).

Now listen to another sample question.:

Sample Answer
Ⓐ Ⓑ Ⓒ ●

In your test book, you read:

(A) It is required of all science majors.
(B) It will never be shown again.
(C) It can help viewers improve their memory skills.
(D) It will help with course work.

The best answer to the question "Why does the speaker recommend watching the program?" is (D), "It will help with course work." Therefore, the correct choice is (D).

Remember, you are **not** allowed to take notes or write in your test book.

39. (A) To introduce a recording of a
Native American legend
   (B) To encourage young people to
become storytellers
   (C) To compare oral and written
traditions
   (D) To tell a famous story

40. (A) They were used to teach children
the language.
   (B) They carried news from one tribe
to another.
   (C) They preserved the society's
history.
   (D) They served as chiefs.

41. (A) They are more comprehensive
than earlier recordings.
   (B) They provide income for the
Crow people.
   (C) Today's children do not enjoy
Native American stories.
   (D) Without recordings the stories
might be forgotten.

42. (A) Children have better memories
than adults do.
   (B) The traditional storytellers have
died.
   (C) He is interested in the children's
reactions.
   (D) The storytellers are too busy to be
interviewed.

43. (A) To prepare students for the next
reading assignment
   (B) To provide background
information for a class discussion
   (C) To review material from a
previous class
   (D) To prepare for a quiz on chapter
six

44. (A) Insurance companies
   (B) Sailors
   (C) Manufacturers
   (D) Merchants

45. (A) The distance the merchandise had
to be shipped
   (B) The number of insurance
companies available at the time
   (C) The amount of danger involved in
shipping the goods
   (D) The type of vessel used to
transport the goods

46. (A) Only four types of policies still
exist today.
   (B) They are cheaper than the ones in
the Middle Ages.
   (C) They include features similar to
earlier policies.
   (D) The interest rates are based on
early methods of calculation.

47. (A) How they enjoy their food
    (B) How they communicate with
        each other
    (C) How they depend on the Sun
    (D) How they learn different dances

48. (A) A signal that it is tired
    (B) A message about a food source
    (C) Acceptance of another honeybee
        to its hive
    (D) A warning that danger is near

49. (A) It is not verbal.
    (B) It is not informative.
    (C) It is not effective.
    (D) It is not complicated.

50. (A) Read the chapters on honeybee
        communication
    (B) Discuss the different ways humans
        communicate
    (C) Give examples of other types of
        animal communication
    (D) Write a paper on the various forms
        of communication

THIS IS THE END OF SECTION 1.

WHEN YOU ARE READY, READ "REVIEW MATERIAL" ON THE NEXT PAGE.

Review Material—Practice Test, Section 1

If you have finished the questions in Section 1 of the practice test and would like to review the Listening Comprehension material, follow these instructions.

- Use the answer key below to determine which questions you answered correctly.

- Restart the audio CD.

- Tear out the Listening Comprehension script. Place the script next to the test questions so you can see the four answer choices,

- Read the script as you listen to the recorded material. It will help you recognize words that you may not have understood correctly.

Section 1 Answer Key

Part A		Part B		Part C	
1.	C	31.	A	39.	A
2.	D	32.	C	40.	C
3.	C	33.	D	41.	D
4.	A	34.	A	42.	B
5.	C	35.	C	43.	B
6.	A	36.	D	44.	D
7.	A	37.	D	45.	C
8.	A	38.	D	46.	C
9.	B			47.	B
10.	A			48.	B
11.	A			49.	A
12.	C			50.	C
13.	D				
14.	D				
15.	D				
16.	B				
17.	C				
18.	D				
19.	D				
20.	C				
21.	D				
22.	A				
23.	A				
24.	C				
25.	A				
26.	D				
27.	B				
28.	C				
29.	C				
30.	D				

Part A

Questions 1–30

1. **Woman:** No, no. I asked you to get me the economics test book, not the textbook.
   Man: Oh, no wonder the cashier looked at me that way.

   Narrator: What can be inferred about the man?

   (C) The woman asked the man to buy a test book. The "not" indicates that the man misunderstood her. In this item it is important to pay attention to the words stressed by the woman.

2. **Man:** You did an excellent job on that presentation.
   Woman: Thanks. I put a lot of time into it.

   Narrator: What does the woman mean?

   (D) The idiom "to put a lot of time into something" means to work hard on something for a long time. The woman is explaining that she worked hard on her presentation.

3. **Man:** I can't find my wallet! And it has more than a hundred dollars in it!
   Woman: Calm down a minute. Have you checked the coat you had on this morning?

   Narrator: What does the woman suggest the man do?

   (C) When the woman asks whether the man has "checked his coat," she is implying that he should look for the wallet in the coat's pockets.

4. **Woman:** I waited for you at the library for more than 30 minutes yesterday. Weren't we supposed to meet at noon?
   Man: Oh that's right! I'm sorry, I've been so wrapped up in my science project it just slipped my mind.

   Narrator: What does the man mean?

   (A) "Slip one's mind" is an idiom meaning to forget to do something; in this case the man forgot to meet the woman at the library. Even if you do not know the meaning of this idiom, you can identify the best answer from the woman's statement that she had waited for the man for more than 30 minutes yesterday.

5. **Woman:** This is the most boring dormitory party I've ever been to.
   Man: It certainly could use some livening up.

   Narrator: What does the man imply?

   (C) The word "it" in the man's statement refers to "the dormitory party." "To liven up" is an idiom meaning to make something more energetic or animated. This statement shows that the man agrees with the woman's opinion that the party is boring.

6. **Man:** I've got three exams tomorrow! I can't possibly study for all of them!
   Woman: I'm just glad I'm not in your shoes!

   Narrator: What does the woman mean?
   (A) "To be in your shoes" is an idiom meaning to be in your situation, so the woman is glad she does not have three exams the next day like the man does.

7. **Woman:** My roommate Karen makes the best salads. I don't understand why mine never taste as good as hers.
   Man: It's not such a mystery—she's a vegetarian and has simply perfected the art.

   Narrator: What does the man mean?

   (A) "To perfect the art" of something means to become an expert at doing it. The man is stating that Karen has made many salads and has become very good at it.

8. **Woman**: Do you think you could help me get a new couch into my apartment this weekend?
   Man: Didn't you make arrangements to have it delivered? That'd be easier and it's free.

   Narrator: What does the man suggest the woman do?

   (A) When the man asks, "Didn't you make arrangements to have it delivered?" and says that delivery is "easier" and "free," he is implying that the woman should ask the store to deliver the couch.

9. **Woman:** The opening of the new photo exhibit was great. I thought you said you were coming, too—to meet the artist.
   Man: [surprised] Oh, no. That was last weekend?

   Narrator: What can be inferred about the man?

   (B) The man's reaction to the woman's statement indicates that he forgot when the exhibit opened.

10. **Woman:** [with disapproval] Are you going to buy that? I'm not sure I like it on you.
    Man: Well, it is comfortable—perfect for our trip. Maybe I'd better find a mirror so I can see how it looks.

    Narrator: What is the man doing?

    (A) The woman's tone indicates that she does not approve of what the man is planning to buy. The word "on" in the woman's statement implies that the man is trying on clothes. The man's statement that he should see how "it looks" on him supports that.

11. **Man:** [grunt of disgust] Ugh, I can't figure out why I can't get my computer to print.
    Woman: Did you check the cables? Sometimes they just get loose.

    Narrator: What does the woman suggest the man do?

    (A) The woman's question, "Did you check the cables?" is an implied suggestion that the man should see if the cables are loose.

12. **Woman:** I'm going out to the golf course this afternoon. Would you like to come along? I could use a few pointers on my game.
Man: I'd be glad to, but I'm not sure what I could show you.

Narrator: What does the man mean?

(C) The word "pointers" means "hints" in this context. The woman is asking the man to help her improve her golf technique. The man implies that he may not be a good enough golf player himself to help her.

13. **Man:** I think I'll take three of these tablets. My head is killing me!
Woman: You'd better read the label carefully first.

Narrator: What does the woman imply the man should do?

(D) The word "dosage" in the answer means the amount, or dose, of a medicine a person should take. The woman implies that the man should check the label on the medicine bottle to make sure he is not taking too many tablets. Her tone of warning reinforces the fact that she is cautioning him.

14. **Man:** I thought you weren't planning to come home for supper.
Woman: Oh, but I was.

Narrator: What does the woman mean?

(D) The woman's use of "but" indicates that she is contradicting the man's statement.

15. **Man:** I'm really looking forward to taking up piano this semester.
Woman: I hope you do better than I did when I took lessons. I just don't have an ear for music.

Narrator: What does the woman mean?

(D) The woman indicates that she did not do well when she studied the piano because she does not "have an ear for music," an idiom meaning that a person has little musical ability. Her hope that the man will play the piano better than she did reinforces this.

16. **Woman:** Did you pick up some French bread at the bakery?
Man: A sign on the window said: "Closed. Please call again."

Narrator: What does the man mean?

(B) In this context "call" means "to come back." A shop that is "closed" is not open for business.

17. **Man:** I'm nervous about the job interview I have this afternoon.
Woman: Relax. Just let them know about your background. It's perfect for the job.

Narrator: What does the woman suggest the man do?

(C) "Background" here means previous experience or training that might qualify a person for a job. The woman is suggesting that the man describe his background at the job interview because he is well qualified.

18. **Man:** I really don't see the value of these modern paintings. They look like the kind of pictures my four-year-old nephew paints.
Woman: And I'll bet he uses brighter colors, too!

Narrator: What can be inferred about the speakers?

(D) By saying that the modern paintings look like pictures made by his nephew, a very young child, the man is implying that he does not think highly of modern art. The woman's use of "And" indicates that she agrees with him. Her reference to brighter colors suggests that she dislikes the muted colors of the paintings.

19. **Man:** Are you flying or taking the train home for the summer?
Woman: Neither. Since I've got this job at the university library, my parents are just going to come visit sometime in July.

Narrator: What does the woman mean?

(D) The woman indicates that she will be working at the university for the summer, and her parents are going to visit her there. She will not be going home.

20. **Woman:** Do you have any idea when tonight's rehearsal will be over?
Man: Beats me. You could try asking Jeff.

Narrator: What does the man mean?

(C) "Beats me" is an idiom meaning "I don't know." The man suggests that the woman ask Jeff, implying that Jeff might know what time the rehearsal ends.

21. **Woman:** The music we were playing last night didn't disturb you, did it?
Man: [sarcastically] I was trying to get some work done.

Narrator: What does the man imply about the music?

(D) The man's tone of voice indicates that he was disturbed by the music, and his statement that he "was trying to get some work done" implies that the music was distracting.

22. **Woman:** The election's tomorrow. Do you want to help me put up some more campaign posters?
Man: I don't see why we should bother. The people who are going to vote have already made up their minds.

Narrator: What does the man imply?

(A) The man suggests that putting up more posters would not be helpful because it is too late to change voters' minds.

23. **Woman:** Jessie's doing well in chemistry now, isn't she?
Man: Yes, she's really come a long way.

Narrator: What does the man say about Jessie?

(A) "Come a long way" is an idiom meaning a lot of progress has been made. The man is stating that Jessie's chemistry work is much improved.

24. *Man:* I give up! I'll never learn how to ski as well as you!
    Woman: Don't be discouraged. Remember, I practically grew up on skis.

    Narrator: What does the woman imply?

    (C) The woman is encouraging the man, who is just learning to ski, and reminding him that she has been skiing a long time ("grew up on skis").

25. *Woman:* Your neighbors used to grow the most wonderful peaches!
    Man: You have a good memory. The tree went down in a storm a few years ago, and I'd completely forgotten about it.

    Narrator: What does the man imply?

    (A) The phase "used to grow" implies that the man's neighbors no longer grow peaches. His statement that the tree is gone reinforces this.

26. *Woman:* Jack's plan to move across the country and start his own business is really brave, but I hope he knows what he's doing.
    Man: Oh, I know. I can't help but wonder how he's ever going to manage it.

    Narrator: What does the man mean?

    (D) "Going to manage" is an idiom meaning "going to succeed at" or "going to handle" something. The phrase "can't help but wonder" implies that the man is wondering about Jack's ability to succeed in the new business.

27. *Man:* I hear that Professor Jones is going to be on the news tonight. Could I come over and watch it?
    Woman: Well, a bunch of us from class are going to [*gonna*] go over to Dave's to watch it. Want to [*Wanna*] join us?

    Narrator: What will the speakers probably do this evening?

    (B) The man wants to watch a television news program at the woman's home, but she indicates she is going to watch it elsewhere with some classmates. She invites the man to join them.

28. *Woman:* I've been combing the classifieds for an apartment.
    Man: I think there're some good rentals on the bulletin board outside the student center.

    Narrator: What does the man suggest the woman do?

    (C) The verb "comb" in this context means to search through something carefully. "Classifieds" is a shortened term for "classified advertisements," which are newspaper listings that include notices about apartments available for rent. The man suggests that the woman look instead at notices posted on campus, particularly on the bulletin board outside the student center.

29. **Woman:** Look at it pour! So much for our tennis game.

Man: Yeah, and since it's supposed to keep up all night, we ought to forget about tomorrow's lunch game too.

Narrator: What does the man imply?

(C) The word "it" refers to the weather, and "pour" is a common idiomatic verb meaning "rain heavily." Since it's going to rain all night, they will not be able to play tennis tomorrow either, because the tennis courts will be too wet.

30. **Man:** The phone will be installed tomorrow.

Woman: Oh, so you _did_ order it.

Narrator: What had the woman assumed?

(D) The woman's comment and tone of voice implies that she did not know that the man had ordered the phone. Note that she says, "Oh, so you _did_ order it," rather than simply, "Oh, so you ordered it." The "did" adds emphasis, suggesting that she had been uncertain until then whether the man had ordered the phone.

Part B

Questions 31–34

Narrator: Listen to part of an interview between a student newspaper reporter and a professor.

Woman: Professor Smith, let me make sure my information is accurate. The title of your book is _Moving People: The New York Subway and Urban Development._ It's 312 pages long, and it will be published next month.

Man: That's right. You should be sure to make clear that I'm not the sole author. My coauthor is Kathleen Douglas.

Woman: Yes. I have that. So why write about the subways?

Man: I'm a cultural historian, and I'm interested in the impact of technology on people's lives. The subways increased everyone's mobility. How cheap, efficient transportation changed life in New York—that's really the focus.

Woman: Have the subways been around a long time?

Man: Some unsuccessful attempts were made as far back as the 1870s, but the history of the subways really begins with the founding of the IRT, the Interborough Rapid Transit Company, in 1900. Today we call it the IRT.

Woman: So the IRT built the first subway in 1900 ?

Man: They started work in 1900, but it took four years to dig the tunnel and lay the track for the first line.

Woman: And it was a success?

Man: Oh, yes. People knew it would transform their lives—a hundred thousand rode the train the first day. I've got some great pictures of that day.

Woman: Are they in the book?

Man: Yes. Those and quite a few others. Actually, Kathleen collected the photographs. I was going over this set when you arrived.

31. *Narrator:* What is the main topic of the interview?

    (A) The speakers are discussing a book that was written by the professor and another author that will be published soon. The student introduces the topic in her opening statements.

32. *Narrator:* Who is Kathleen Douglas?

    (C) The professor identifies Kathleen Douglas as his coauthor in his first reply to the student. He also refers to her work on the book's photographs at the end of the conversation.

33. *Narrator:* What aspect of the New York subway especially interests the professor?

    (D) In the fourth exchange, the professor says he is interested in the impact of technology on people's lives. (D) is a paraphrase of this statement.

34. *Narrator:* What will the professor probably do next?

    (A) At the end of the interview, the speakers are discussing some photographs for the book. The professor says he was going over them when the woman arrived. It would be natural for the professor to go on to show the photographs to the woman.

Questions 35–38

Narrator: Listen to a conversation between two students who are members of the computer club.

Man: Sorry to say this, Pam, but I think we're going to [*gonna*] have to [*hafta*] cancel tonight's planning meeting.

Woman: You're kidding, Tom. With the computer fair only two weeks away? Is the weather that bad?

Man: Well, I just listened to the noon forecast on the radio, and the snow's supposed to start between 2:00 [*two*] and 3:00 [*three*] and continue throughout the afternoon and evening. Some other campus clubs have already announced they're not meeting.

Woman: Gee . . . I'd hate to cancel, though . . . There's so much to do to get ready.

Man: I know what you mean, but if the weather's bad, we probably wouldn't get much of a turnout anyway. Remember how many computer club members live far from campus.

Woman: Maybe you're right. And Kathy told me yesterday that the publicity's all taken care of . . .

Man: And I've made the arrangements for the rooms we'll be using, so that's all set, too.

Woman: Sounds as if we're further ahead than I thought Maybe we could just postpone the meeting till tomorrow night.

Man: I think we'd better wait a couple of [*couple' a*] days until the roads clear. How about the day after tomorrow? I could get on the phone and let everyone know.

Woman: I'll split the list with you. That way we'll each have only ten calls to make.

Man: Great. And when I talk to Sara, I'll find out how the response from the computer vendors has been.

Woman: Last I heard, there were about twenty software companies coming.

Man: I guess everything's coming along all right then. Let's just hope we have good weather the day of the fair.

35. *Narrator:* What are the speakers working on?

   (C) This is a gist question. The speakers, both students in a computer club, are discussing plans for an upcoming computer fair. The man's opening lines refer to their "planning meeting," and much of the discussion refers to specific activities that have been done in anticipation of an upcoming event (publicity, arrangements for rooms, participation by software companies). At the very end of the conversation the man refers to "the day of the fair," which tells us what the event is.

36. *Narrator:* Why do the speakers decide to cancel the meeting?

   (D) The conversation begins with the speakers discussing the approaching storm and whether they should cancel the meeting. The man expresses concern that people might not be able to attend due to the bad weather. The speakers also talk about the length of the snowstorm and how long it will be "until the roads clear."

37. *Narrator:* Where is the planning meeting scheduled to take place?

   (D) The man says that many club members "live far from campus," so we can infer that the meeting will take place on campus.

38. *Narrator:* How are the speakers going to let club members know about the change in plans?

   (D) Near the end of the conversation the man says he will call the club members and let them know about the rescheduled meeting. The woman then offers to call some of the club members for him.

Part C

Questions 39–42

Narrator: Listen to a talk by an anthropologist.

Man: To continue our series of recordings from the museum's archives, this afternoon you will have the opportunity to hear a preeminent Native American storyteller, Joseph Medicine Crow. This museum is fortunate to have some of the recordings of legends and other stories he has collected from his native Crow culture, which is one of the Plains Indian groups.

To understand the significance of these recordings, it is important to remember that the history and traditions of Native Americans were not written down. Instead they were passed down from one generation to the next by tribal storytellers. Often these storytellers were specially trained. They were chosen for the role when young and charged with remembering and sharing their people's oral history—a tradition that no longer exists.

Joseph Medicine Crow recorded and saved the stories of his grandfather, one of the Crow people's last war chiefs. He also collected the memoirs of other tribal elders. Today, the traditional tribal storytellers Joseph Crow knew as a young man are all gone, so he must now gather information from their children and grandchildren.

Now we'll hear a tape of this great storyteller as he recounts a legend of the Crow people. The slides you will see accompanying this story are pictures of artifacts of various Plains Indian cultures.

39. *Narrator:* What is the speaker's main purpose?

   (A) At the beginning of the talk, the speaker says that the presentation is part of "a series of recordings," and that today the audience will hear from a Native American storyteller.

40. *Narrator:* Why were storytellers important to Plains Indian cultures?

   (C) The speaker says that the history and traditions of Native Americans were not preserved in any written form. Instead they were passed down from one generation to another by storytellers of the tribes. This explains why the storytellers are important.

41. *Narrator:* According to the talk, why are Joseph Medicine Crow's recordings especially important now?

   (D) The speaker explains that Joseph Medicine Crow collected stories from his grandfather and other tribal elders who are no longer living. Their children and grandchildren have not been trained to be storytellers, so they might not remember all the stories. This suggests that Joseph Medicine Crow's recordings are an important source of the traditional stories.

42. *Narrator:* Why does Joseph Medicine Crow collect material from storytellers' children?

   (B) The speaker indicates the storytellers and tribal elders are no longer living. The storytellers' children are the only remaining source of the oral history.

Narrator: Listen to a professor in a business class.

Woman: I hope you've all finished reading the assigned chapter on insurance—so that you're prepared for our discussion today. But, before we start, I'd like to mention a few things your text doesn't go into.

It's interesting to note that insurance has existed in some form for a very long time. The earliest insurance policies were what were called bottomry contracts. They provided shipping protection for merchants as far back as 3000 B.C.E.

In general, the contracts were often no more than verbal agreements. They granted loans to merchants with the understanding that if a particular shipment of goods was lost at sea, the loan didn't have to be repaid. Interest on the loans varied according to how risky it was to transport the goods. During periods of heavy piracy at sea, for example, the amount of interest and the cost of the policy went up considerably.

So, you can see how insurance helped encourage international trade. Even the most cautious merchants became willing to risk shipping their goods over long distances—not to mention in hazardous weather conditions—when they had this kind of protection available.

Generally speaking, the basic form of an insurance policy has been pretty much the same since the Middle Ages. There are four points that were salient then and remain paramount in all policies today. These were outlined in chapter six and will serve as the basis for the rest of today's discussion. Can anyone tell me what one of those points might be?

43. *Narrator:* What is the purpose of the professor's talk?

   (B) The professor indicates she will talk about additional information that is not in the students' textbook before beginning the class discussion.

44. *Narrator:* Who were the first insurance contracts designed to protect?

   (D) The professor says that the earliest insurance policies, called bottomry contracts, provided protection for merchants.

45. *Narrator:* What does the professor say determined the cost of early insurance policies?

   (C) The professor explains that early insurance policies were loans. The interest that was charged varied according to the amount of risk involved in shipping the goods. The price was determined by the anticipated dangers of the journey. She gives the danger of piracy as an example of a risk that could increase the insurance.

46. *Narrator:* What does the professor say about current insurance policies?

   (C) The professor says that policies have remained pretty much the same since the Middle Ages, so their features are similar.

Narrator: Listen to part of a talk about honeybees.

Woman: Communication—what is communication? Some of you will say it is language. But is communication just limited to human language? You might be surprised to learn that scientists have discovered that honeybees have a form of communication that is as complicated and as effective as human language. Honeybees communicate by dancing. For example, when a honeybee finds food it returns to its hive and performs a dance. This dance communicates a message about the food. Basically, there are three types of dances: the round dance, the sickle dance, and the tail-wagging dance. In all three dances, the number of turns in the bee's dance tells the other bees how far the food is from the hive. The angle of the bee's dance in relation to the Sun tells the direction of food from the hive.

So you see, honeybees communicate using one form of nonverbal communication. Can anyone suggest another form of nonverbal communication used by animals?

47. *Narrator:* What aspect of honeybees does the speaker discuss?

   (B) The speaker discusses "communication" at the beginning and then refers to how honeybees communicate with one another.

48. *Narrator:* According to the speaker, what does the honeybee communicate through its dances?

   (B) The speaker mentions several times that the dance communicates information about the location of food.

49. *Narrator:* What does the speaker say about the honeybee's system of communication?

   (A) In summarizing the talk, the speaker indicates that honeybees communicate nonverbally.

50. *Narrator:* What does the speaker ask the listeners to do at the end of the talk?

   (C) At the end of the talk, the speaker asks for additional examples of types of nonverbal communication in animals.

Section 2

Structure and Written Expression

Time: 25 minutes (including the reading of the directions)

Now set your clock for 25 minutes.

The Structure and Written Expression section is designed to measure your ability to recognize language that is appropriate for standard written English. There are two types of questions in this section, with special directions for each type.

Structure

Directions: Questions 1–15 are incomplete sentences. Beneath each sentence you will see four words or phrases, marked (A), (B), (C), and (D). Choose the one word or phrase that best completes the sentence. Then, on your answer sheet, find the number of the question and fill in the space that corresponds to the letter of the answer you have chosen.

Example I

Sample Answer

Geysers have often been compared to volcanoes ------- both emit hot liquids from below Earth's surface.

    (A) despite
    (B) because
    (C) in regard to
    (D) as a result of

The sentence should read: "Geysers have often been compared to volcanoes because both emit hot liquids from below Earth's surface." Therefore, you should choose (B).

Example II

Sample Answer

During the early period of ocean navigation, ------- any need for sophisticated instruments and techniques.

    (A) so that hardly
    (B) when there hardly was
    (C) hardly was
    (D) there was hardly

The sentence should read: "During the early period of ocean navigation, there was hardly any need for sophisticated instruments and techniques." Therefore, you should choose (D).

NOW BEGIN WORK ON THE QUESTIONS.

1. Simple photographic lenses cannot ------- sharp, undistorted images over a wide field.

   (A) to form
   (B) are formed
   (C) forming
   (D) form

2. Of all the factors affecting agricultural yields, weather is the one ------- the most.

   (A) it influences farmers
   (B) that influences farmers
   (C) farmers that it influences
   (D) why farmers influence it

3. Beverly Sills, -------, assumed directorship of the New York City Opera in 1979.

   (A) be a star soprano
   (B) was a star soprano
   (C) a star soprano and
   (D) a star soprano

4. ------- of tissues is known as histology.

   (A) Studying scientific
   (B) The scientific study
   (C) To study scientifically
   (D) That is scientific studying

5. With the exception of mercury, ------- at standard temperature and pressure.

   (A) the metallic elements are solid
   (B) which is a solid metallic element
   (C) metallic elements being solid
   (D) since the metallic elements are solid

6. Dehydration is ------- that a land animal faces.

   (A) the often greatest hazard
   (B) the greatest often hazard
   (C) often the greatest hazard
   (D) often the hazard greatest

7. By tracking the eye of a hurricane, forecasters can determine the speed at which -------.

   (A) is a storm moving
   (B) a storm is moving
   (C) is moving a storm
   (D) a moving storm

8. The publication of *Adventures of Huckleberry Finn* helped make Mark Twain one of America's ------- literary figures.

   (A) most famous
   (B) the most famous
   (C) are most famous
   (D) and most famous

9. Technology will play a key role in ------- future lifestyles.

   (A) to shape
   (B) shaping
   (C) shape of
   (D) shaped

10. The computer has dramatically affected ------- many products are designed.

    (A) is the way
    (B) that the way
    (C) which way do
    (D) the way

11. The early railroads were ------- the existing arteries of transportation: roads, turnpikes, and canals and other waterways.

    (A) those short lines connected
    (B) short lines that connected
    (C) connected by short lines
    (D) short connecting lines

12. ------- as a masterpiece, a work of art must transcend the ideals of the period in which it was created.

    (A) Ranks
    (B) The ranking
    (C) To be ranked
    (D) For being ranked

13. Jackie Robinson, ------- to play baseball in the major leagues, joined the Brooklyn Dodgers in 1947.

    (A) the African American who first
    (B) the first African American
    (C) was the first African American
    (D) the first and an African American who

14. During the flood of 1927, the Red Cross, ------- out of emergency headquarters in Mississippi, set up temporary shelters for the homeless.

    (A) operates
    (B) is operating
    (C) has operated
    (D) operating

15. In bacteria and in other organisms, ------- is DNA that provides the genetic information.

    (A) both
    (B) which
    (C) and
    (D) it

SECTION 2 CONTINUES ON THE NEXT PAGE.

Written Expression

Directions: In questions 16–40, each sentence has four underlined words or phrases. The four underlined parts of the sentence are marked (A), (B), (C), and (D). Choose the one underlined word or phrase that must be changed for the sentence to be correct. Then, on your answer sheet, find the number of the question and fill in the space that corresponds to the letter of the answer you have chosen.

Example I

Sample Answer
● Ⓑ Ⓒ Ⓓ

Guppies are sometimes <u>call</u> rainbow <u>fish</u> <u>due</u> to the <u>bright</u> colors of the males.
               A   B C   D

The sentence should read: "Guppies are sometimes called rainbow fish due to the bright colors of the males." Therefore, you should choose (A).

Example II

Sample Answer
Ⓐ ● Ⓒ Ⓓ

<u>Serving</u> several <u>term</u> in the United States Congress, Shirley Chisholm became a <u>respected</u>
  A   B   C
United States <u>politician</u>.
                    D

The sentence should read: "Serving several terms in the United States Congress, Shirley Chisholm became a respected United States politician" Therefore, you should choose (B).

NOW BEGIN WORK ON THE QUESTIONS.

16. Twenty to <u>thirty year</u> after a mature forest <u>is cleared away</u>, a <u>nearly</u> impenetrable
               A   B   C

    thicket of trees and shrubs <u>develops</u>.
                          D

17. The <u>first</u> national park <u>in world</u>, Yellowstone National Park, <u>was</u> established <u>in</u> 1872.
      A   B   C   D

18. <u>Because</u> it does not have a blood <u>supply</u>, the cornea takes <u>their</u> oxygen <u>directly</u> from
   A   B   C   D

    the air.

19. Magnificent <u>mountains</u> and <u>coastal</u> scenery <u>is</u> British Columbia's <u>chief</u> tourist
              A   B   C   D

    attractions.

20. Scientists at <u>universities</u> are <u>often</u> more <u>involved</u> in theoretical research than in
               A   B   C

    <u>practically</u> research.
     D

21. John Rosamond Johnson <u>he composed</u> numerous <u>songs</u>, <u>including</u> *Lift Every Voice*
                              A   B   C

    and Sing, <u>for which</u> his brother, James Weldon Johnson, wrote the words.
             D

22. Nylon, a synthetic material <u>done</u> from a <u>combination</u> of water, air, and a by-product
                                  A   B

    of coal, was first <u>introduced</u> in 1938.
  <u></u>C   D

   (*of coal* C underlined)

23. Ornithology, the study of birds, is one of the <u>major</u> scientific <u>fields</u> in which amateurs
                                                 A   B

    <u>play</u> a role in accumulating, researching, and <u>publish</u> data.
   C   D

24. Animation is a <u>technique</u> for <u>creativity</u> the illusion <u>of life</u> in inanimate <u>things</u>.
                 A   B   C   D

25. The nonviolent protest advocated <u>by</u> Dr. Martin Luther King, Jr., <u>proving</u> highly
                              A   B

    effective in an age of <u>expanding</u> television news <u>coverage</u>.
                     C   D

26. <u>On</u> December 7, 1787, Delaware <u>became a</u> first state <u>to ratify</u> the United
   A   B C   D

    States Constitution.

27. <u>Nutritionists</u> believe <u>what</u> diet affects <u>how</u> one feels <u>physically</u> and emotionally.
     A   B   C   D

28. Mealii Kalama, creator of <u>over</u> 400 Hawaiian quilts, <u>was granted</u> a National Heritage
                       A   B
Fellowship in 1985 for <u>herself</u> <u>contributions</u> to folk art.
                    C   D

29. A jetty <u>serves</u> to define and deepen <u>a channel</u>, improve <u>navigate</u>, or protect <u>a harbor</u>.
         A   B   C   D

30. Minoru Yamasaki achieved a reputation as an architect <u>which</u> works <u>departed from</u>
                                         A   B
the austerity <u>frequently</u> associated <u>with</u> architecture after the Second World War.
               C   D

31. Chemical research <u>provides</u> information that is useful <u>when</u> the <u>textile</u> industry in the
                     A   B   C
<u>development</u> of new fabrics.
   D

32. Because of <u>its</u> vast tracts of <u>virtually</u> uninhabited northern forest, Canada has <u>one</u> of
            A   B   C
the lowest population <u>density</u> in the world.
                  D

33. Bromyrite crystals <u>have</u> a diamond-like luster and are usually <u>colorless</u>, but they <u>dark</u>
              A   B   C
to brown when <u>exposed</u> to light.
          D

34. <u>Stars</u> in our universe vary <u>in</u> temperature, color, <u>bright</u>, size, and <u>mass</u>.
   A   B   C   D

35. Ice is less <u>denser</u> <u>than</u> the liquid <u>from which</u> <u>it</u> is formed.
          A B   C   D

36. The 1983 Nobel Prize in Medicine <u>was awarded</u> to Barbara McClintock for her
                             A
<u>experiments with</u> maize and her <u>discoveries</u> <u>regardless</u> the nature of DNA.
      B   C   D

37. <u>In</u> 1866 to 1883, the bison population in North America <u>was reduced</u> from an
A   B
<u>estimated</u> 13 million to a few <u>hundred</u>.
    C   D

38. Most of the <u>damage property</u> attributed <u>to</u> the San Francisco earthquake <u>of</u> 1906
      A   B   C

 resulted from the fire <u>that followed</u>.
          D

39. James Baldwin's plays and short stories, <u>which are</u> to <u>some degree</u> autobiographical,
                   A   B

 established <u>them</u> as a <u>leading</u> figure in the United States civil rights movement.
      C   D

40. Thunder can be <u>listened</u> from a <u>maximum</u> distance of about ten miles <u>except</u> under
        A   B   C

 <u>unusual</u> atmospheric conditions.
  D

Practice Section 2 Review Material

If you have finished the questions in Practice Section 2 and would like to review the Structure and Written Expression material, follow these instructions.

Use the answer key below to determine which questions you answered correctly and incorrectly. Then read the following explanations for the correct answers.

Section 2 Answer Key

Structure		Written Expression	
1.	D	16.	A
2.	B	17.	B
3.	D	18.	C
4.	B	19.	C
5.	A	20.	D
6.	C	21.	A
7.	B	22.	A
8.	A	23.	D
9.	B	24.	B
10.	D	25.	B
11.	B	26.	C
12.	C	27.	B
13.	B	28.	C
14.	D	29	C
15.	D	30.	A
		31.	B
		32.	D
		33.	C
		34.	C
		35.	A
		36.	D
		37.	A
		38.	A
		39.	C
		40.	A

EXPLANATIONS FOR CORRECT ANSWERS

Structure

1. **(D)** After any modal verb (such as "can"), the simple form of the verb, in this case "form," must be used. This is always the case with modals, even with the negative forms, such as "cannot."

2. **(B)** The relative (adjective) clause "that influences farmers the most" modifies the pronoun "one." The other choices do not modify the pronoun.

3. **(D)** A noun phrase that is an appositive is needed to fill the blank. Only "a star soprano" does that.

4. **(B)** "The scientific study of tissues" is the only noun phrase that can act as the subject of this sentence.

5. **(A)** A subject and verb are required to complete the main clause.

6. **(C)** This question tests the ability to recognize correct word order. The adverb "often" must immediately follow the verb "is," and the adjective "greatest" must precede the noun "hazard." Only (C) has the words in the correct order.

7. **(B)** This question tests the structure of the relative (adjective) clause that is introduced by "at which." (B) is correct because it contains a subject and verb presented in the right order.

8. **(A)** After the possessive noun "America's," the adjective phrase "most famous" is correct. Although choice (B) is also an adjective phrase, the use of "the" after a possessive noun is not correct.

9. **(B)** When the preposition "in" is followed by a verb, the verb must be in the "-ing" (gerund) form.

10. **(D)** In this sentence, an object is required after the active form of the verb "affected." Here the noun phrase "the way" serves as the object and is correctly modified by the relative (adjective) clause, "many products are designed."

11. **(B)** Following the verb "were," a noun phrase that means the same thing as the subject, "The early railroads," is used. A relative pronoun ("that") and a verb ("connected") are needed to introduce the relative (adjective) clause that follows.

12. **(C)** The infinitive form of the verb is the only choice that completes this sentence grammatically. In this sentence, "to" of the infinitive is a shortened form of "in order to."

13. **(B)** A noun phrase, set off by commas, follows the subject and identifies the subject. Only choice (B) completes the noun phrase grammatically.

14. **(D)** "Operating," a participle, introduces an adjective phrase that modifies "Red Cross."

15. **(D)** "DNA" is the delayed subject of the sentence, and "it" is necessary to fill the subject space before the verb.

Written Expression

16. **(A)** "Thirty" is plural; therefore, "year" must be plural.

17. **(B)** "The" is needed before the specific noun "world."

18. **(C)** "Its" must be used instead of "their" because "cornea" is singular.

19. **(C)** There are two subjects, "mountains" and "scenery," so the verb must be corrected to "are."

20. **(D)** The adjective form "practical" should be used to modify the noun "research."

21. **(A)** "John Rosamond Johnson" is the subject of the verb "composed"; the pronoun "he" is unnecessary and ungrammatically repeats the subject.

22. **(A)** "Done" is the wrong word choice; it should be "made."

23. **(D)** "Publishing" must be used to be parallel to the other "-ing" forms in the series.

24. **(B)** The gerund form "creating" is needed after "for."

25. **(B)** This sentence needs a main finite verb; "proving" must be changed to "proved."

26. **(C)** "The" must be used before the definite noun phrase "first state."

27. **(B)** "That," not "what," must introduce the noun clause that begins with "diet affects."

28. **(C)** The possessive adjective "her" should be used to modify "contributions," not the reflexive pronoun "herself."

29. **(C)** The noun "navigation" should be used, since it is the object of the verb "improve" and parallel to the nouns "channel" and "harbor."

30. **(A)** The possessive relative pronoun "whose" must be used because the relative (adjective) clause describes a possessive relationship.

31. **(B)** "When" is the wrong word choice; "for," or another appropriate preposition, must be used after "useful."

32. **(D)** A plural noun is required to complete a phrase that begins with "one of the."

33. **(C)** After the subject pronoun, "they," there must be the finite verb, "darken," to complete the independent clause.

34. **(C)** The noun form "brightness" is required after the preposition "in," as in the parallel words "size" and "mass."

35. **(A)** The comparative with "less" requires the simple form of the adjective, "dense," not the "-er" form.

36. **(D)** "Regardless" is the wrong word choice; "regarding" is correct.

37. **(A)** "In" is the wrong preposition; "from" should be used with "to" to indicate a span of time between two dates.

38. **(A)** The word order is incorrect here; "property" modifies "damage" and must be placed before "damage."

39. **(C)** The plural pronoun "them" is incorrect; the singular pronoun "him" should be used to refer to "James Baldwin."

40. **(A)** "Listened" is the wrong word choice; "heard" would be used in this context.

Section 3

Reading Comprehension

Time: 55 minutes

Now set your clock for 55 minutes. You have 5 minutes to read the directions.

Directions: In the Reading Comprehension section, you will read several passages. Each one is followed by a number of questions about it. For questions 1–50, you are to choose the one best answer—(A), (B), (C), or (D)—to each question. Then, on your answer sheet, find the number of the question and fill in the space that corresponds to the letter of the answer you have chosen.

Answer all questions about the information in a passage on the basis of what is stated or implied in that passage.

Read the following passage:

> The railroad was not the first institution to impose regularity on society or to draw attention to the importance of precise timekeeping. For as long as merchants have set out their wares at daybreak and communal festivities have been celebrated,
> *Line* people have been in rough agreement with their neighbors as to the time of day. The
> (5) value of this tradition is today more apparent than ever. Were it not for public acceptance of a single yardstick of time, social life would be unbearably chaotic; the massive daily transfers of goods, services, and information would proceed in fits and starts; the very fabric of modern society would begin to unravel.

Example I

Sample Answer

What is the main idea of the passage?

- (A) In modern society we must make more time for our neighbors.
- (B) The traditions of society are timeless.
- (C) An accepted way of measuring time is essential for the smooth functioning of society.
- (D) Society judges people by the times at which they conduct certain activities.

The main idea of the passage is that societies need to agree about how time is to be measured in order to function smoothly. Therefore, you should choose (C).

Example II

In line 5, the phrase "this tradition" refers to

    (A) the practice of starting the business day at dawn

    (B) friendly relations between neighbors

    (C) the railroad's reliance on time schedules

    (D) people's agreement on the measurement of time

The phrase "this tradition" refers to the preceding clause, "people have been in rough agreement with their neighbors as to the time of day." Therefore, you should choose (D).

NOW BEGIN WORK ON THE QUESTIONS.

Questions 1–10

In past centuries, Native Americans living in the arid areas of what is now the
southwestern United States relied on a variety of strategies to ensure the success of
their agriculture. First and foremost, water was the critical factor. The soil was rich
Line because there was little rain to leach out the minerals, but the low precipitation caused
(5) its own problems. Long periods of drought could have made agriculture impossible; on
the other hand, a sudden flood could just as easily have destroyed a crop.

Several techniques were developed to solve the water problem. The simplest was to
plant crops in the floodplains and wait for the annual floods to water the young crops.
A less dangerous technique was to build dikes or dams to control the flooding. These
(10) dikes both protected the plants against excessive flooding and prevented the water from
escaping too quickly once it had arrived. The Hopi people designed their fields in a
checkerboard pattern, with many small dikes, each enclosing only one or two stalks of
maize (corn), while other groups built a series of dams to control the floods. A third
technique was to dig irrigation ditches to bring water from the rivers. Water was
(15) sometimes carried to the fields in jars, particularly if the season was dry. Some crops
were planted where they could be watered directly by the runoff from cliff walls.

Another strategy Native Americans used to ensure a continuous food supply was to
plant their crops in more than one place, hoping that if one crop failed, another would
survive. However, since the soil was rich and not easily exhausted, the same patch of
(20) ground could be cultivated year after year, whereas in the woodlands of the eastern
United States it was necessary to abandon a plot of ground after a few years of farming.
In the Southwest, often two successive crops were planted each year.

It was a common southwestern practice to grow enough food so that some could be
dried and stored for emergencies. If emergency supplies ran low, the people turned to
(25) the local wild plants. If these failed, they moved up into the mountains to gather the
wild plants that might have survived in the cooler atmosphere.

1. What does the passage mainly discuss?

    (A) Agricultural methods of Native Americans
    (B) Irrigation techniques used by the Hopi
    (C) Soil quality in the American Southwest
    (D) Native American methods of storing emergency food supplies

2. The word "solve" in line 7 is closest in meaning to

    (A) advance toward
    (B) protect from
    (B) keep in
    (D) deal with

3. Planting in the floodplains was not ideal because

    (A) the amount of water could not be controlled
    (B) the crops could be eaten by wild animals
    (C) the floodplains were too remote to be cultivated frequently
    (D) corn grows better at high elevations

4. The word "enclosing" in line 12 is closest in meaning to

    (A) defending
    (B) measuring
    (C) surrounding
    (D) extending

5. The word "they" in line 16 refers to

    (A) fields
    (B) jars
    (C) crops
    (D) walls

6. Why did farmers in the Southwest plant crops in several places at the same time?

    (A) They moved frequently from one place to another.
    (B) They feared that one of the crops might fail.
    (C) The size of each field was quite limited.
    (D) They wanted to avoid overusing the soil.

7. The word "patch" in line 19 is closest in meaning to

    (A) type
    (B) level
    (C) group
    (D) piece

8. Why did farmers in the eastern woodlands periodically abandon their fields?

    (A) Seasonal flooding made agriculture impossible.
    (B) They experienced water shortages.
    (C) They wanted a longer growing season.
    (D) The minerals in the soil were exhausted.

9. What did farmers in the Southwest do when a crop failed?

    (A) They planted in the eastern woodlands.
    (B) They gathered food from wild plants.
    (C) They moved away from the mountains.
    (D) They redesigned their fields for the next season.

10. Farmers in the Southwest would have benefited most from which of the following?

    (A) Steeper cliff walls
    (B) More sunshine
    (C) Regular rain
    (D) Smaller dikes

Questions 11–20

Marianne Moore (1887–1972) once said that her writing could be called poetry only because there was no other name for it. Indeed her poems appear to be extremely compressed essays that happen to be printed in jagged lines on the page. Her subjects were varied: animals,
Line laborers, artists, and the craft of poetry. From her general reading came quotations that she
(5) found striking or insightful. She included these in her poems, scrupulously enclosed in quotation marks, and sometimes identified in footnotes. Of this practice, she wrote, "'Why the many quotation marks?' I am asked . . .When a thing has been said so well that it could not be said better, why paraphrase it? Hence my writing is, if not a cabinet of fossils, a kind of collection of flies in amber." Close observation and concentration on detail are the methods of her poetry.

(10) Marianne Moore grew up in Kirkwood, Missouri, near St. Louis. After graduation from Bryn Mawr College in 1909, she taught commercial subjects at the Indian School in Carlisle, Pennsylvania. Later she became a librarian in New York City. During the 1920s she was editor of *The Dial*, an important literary magazine of the period. She lived quietly all her life, mostly in Brooklyn, New York. She spent a lot of time at the Bronx Zoo, fascinated by animals.
(15) Her admiration of the Brooklyn Dodgers baseball team—before the team moved to Los Angeles— was widely known.

Her first book of poems was published in London in 1921 by a group of friends associated with the Imagist movement. From that time on her poetry has been read with interest by succeeding generations of poets and readers. In 1952 she was awarded the Pulitzer Prize for her
(20) *Collected Poems*. She wrote that she did not write poetry "for money or fame. To earn a living is needful, but it can be done in routine ways. One writes because one has a burning desire to objectify what it is indispensable to one's happiness to express."

11. What is the passage mainly about?

    (A) The influence of the Imagists on Marianne Moore
    (B) Essayists and poets of the 1920s
    (C) The use of quotations in poetry
    (D) Marianne Moore's life and work

12. Which of the following can be inferred about Moore's poems?

    (A) They are better known in Europe than the United States.
    (B) They do not use traditional verse forms.
    (C) They were all published in *The Dial*.
    (D) They tend to be abstract.

13. According to the passage, Moore wrote about all of the following EXCEPT

    (A) artists
    (B) animals
    (C) fossils
    (D) workers

14. What does Moore refer to as "flies in amber" (line 9) ?

    (A) A common image in her poetry
    (B) Poetry in the twentieth century
    (C) Concentration on detail
    (D) Quotations within her poetry

15. The author mentions all of the following as jobs held by Moore EXCEPT

    (A) commercial artist
    (B) teacher
    (C) magazine editor
    (D) librarian

16. The word "period" in line 13 is closest in meaning to

    (A) movement
    (B) school
    (C) region
    (D) time

17. Where did Moore spend most of her adult life?

    (A) In Kirkwood
    (B) In Brooklyn
    (C) In Los Angeles
    (D) In Carlisle

18. The word "succeeding" in line 19 is closest in meaning to

    (A) inheriting
    (B) prospering
    (C) diverse
    (D) later

19. The word "it" in line 21 refers to

    (A) writing poetry
    (B) becoming famous
    (C) earning a living
    (D) attracting readers

20. It can be inferred from the passage that Moore wrote because she

    (A) wanted to win awards
    (B) was dissatisfied with what others
    (C) felt a need to express herself
    (D) wanted to raise money for the Bronx Zoo

Questions 21–30

Different fish species swim in different ways. Beginning in the 1920s, careful efforts have been made to classify and measure these various means of locomotion. Although the nomenclature and mathematics used to describe fish locomotion have *Line* become quite complex, the basic classification system is still largely the same as it was (5) first outlined.

The simplest type of swim is "eel-form" (technically, "anguilliform," after the common eel *Anguilla*). As the name suggests, this swimming motion involves undulations, or wavelike motions, of the whole length of the fish's body, the amplitude of the undulation increasing toward the tail. These undulating motions generate a (10) backward thrust of the body against the water, thereby driving it forward. Eel-form swimming is effective but not particularly efficient because the undulations increase the drag, or resistance in the water. It is employed, therefore, mostly by bottom dwellers that do not move quickly or efficiently. Not only eels but also blennies swim this way, as do flounders, which undulate vertically, top to bottom, rather than (15) horizontally, and certain slow-moving sharks, such as the nurse and wobbegong shark.

Most roaming predators display "jack-form" swimming (technically, "carangiform," after the Carangidae family, which includes jacks, scads, and pompanos). Although there is some variation, in general they have certain features in common: a head like the nose of an aircraft, often sloping down on the top, and a tapered posterior that ends (20) in a forked tail. That portion of the body that connects with the forked tail is narrowed. A jack, like other carangiform swimmers, is adapted for acceleration. It thrusts its rather stiff body from side to side, creating propulsion without much waving of the body, encountering less resistance than eel-form undulations produce. The forked pattern of the tail reduces drag; the narrowed portion of the body connected to the tail (25) minimizes recoil, and thus helps keep the body still. Jack-form fish are efficient swimmers, as they must be to catch their prey.

The least efficient swimmers are those that move trunkfish style (technically, "ostraciform," after the family Ostraciidae, which includes trunkfishes and cowfishes). Like the jacks, they use their tails for propulsion, but in so inept and clumsy a manner (30) as to make it clear that speed is not their objective. Puffer fish and porcupine fish swim in trunkfish style. Lacking speed, they must depend on body armor or the secretion of toxic substances for protection.

21. The word "suggests" in line 7 is closest in meaning to

    (A) implies
    (B) demands
    (C) describes
    (D) compares

22. The word "it" in line 10 refers to

    (A) tail
    (B) thrust
    (C) body
    (D) water

23. Which of the following does the author mention as the cause of the eel's inefficient swimming style?

    (A) The increased drag produced by the movement of the body
    (B) The eel's habit of usually swimming near the bottom of the water
    (C) The simple structure of the eel's body
    (D) The weakness of the backward thrust of the eel's tail

24. The word "employed" in line 12 is closest in meaning to

    (A) used
    (B) occupied
    (C) developed
    (D) provided

25. It can be inferred from the passage that blennies (line 13) are

    (A) bottom dwellers
    (B) sharks
    (C) predators
    (D) a type of eel

26. The word "minimizes" in line 25 is closest in meaning to

    (A) prevents
    (B) reduces
    (C) determines
    (D) repeats

27. What does the author mention about fish that are "jack-form" swimmers?

    (A) They usually prey on bottom-dwelling fish.
    (B) Their swimming style lets them catch prey effectively.
    (C) They have tails similar to those of eels.
    (D) Their highly flexible skeletal structure allows them to swim efficiently.

28. The word "objective" in line 30 is closest in meaning to

    (A) ability
    (B) preference
    (C) purpose
    (D) method

29. Which of the following fish would most likely emit a poisonous substance?

    (A) A nurse shark
    (B) A jack
    (C) A pompano
    (D) A puffer fish

30. Which of the following statements does the passage support?

    (A) A scientist today would use a system of classification for fish locomotion similar to that used in the 1920s.
    (B) Scientists today still do not understand the mechanics of fish locomotion.
    (C) Mathematical analysis of fish locomotion has remained largely unaltered since the 1920s.
    (D) The classification of fish locomotion has been simplified since it was devised in the 1920s.

Questions 31–40

People appear to be born to compute. The numerical skills of children develop so early and so inexorably that it is easy to imagine an internal clock of mathematical maturity guiding their growth. Not long after learning to walk and talk, they can set the table with impressive
Line accuracy—one plate, one knife, one spoon, one fork, for each of the five chairs. Soon they are
(5) capable of noting that they have placed five knives, spoons, and forks on the table and, a bit later, that this amounts to fifteen pieces of silverware. Having thus mastered addition, they move on to subtraction. It seems almost reasonable to expect that if a child were secluded on a desert island at birth and retrieved seven years later, he or she could enter a second-grade mathematics class without any serious problems of intellectual adjustment.

(10) Of course, the truth is not so simple. In the twentieth century, the work of cognitive psychologists illuminated the subtle forms of daily learning on which intellectual progress depends. Children were observed as they slowly grasped—or, as the case might be, bumped into—concepts that adults take for granted, as they refused, for instance, to concede that quantity is unchanged as water pours from a short stout glass into a tall thin one. Psychologists have since demonstrated
(15) that young children, asked to count the pencils in a pile, readily report the number of blue or red pencils but must be coaxed into finding the total. Such studies have suggested that the rudiments of mathematics are mastered gradually and with effort. They have also suggested that the very concept of abstract numbers—the idea of a oneness, a twoness, a threeness that applies to any class of objects and is a prerequisite for doing anything more mathematically
(20) demanding than setting a table—is itself far from innate.

31. What does the passage mainly discuss?

    (A) Trends in teaching mathematics to children
    (B) The use of mathematics in child psychology
    (C) The development of mathematical ability in children
    (D) The fundamental concepts of mathematics that children must learn

32. It can be inferred from the passage that children normally learn simple counting

    (A) soon after they learn to talk
    (B) by looking at the clock
    (C) when they begin to be mathematically mature
    (D) after they reach second grade in school

33. The word "illuminated" in line 11 is closest in meaning to

    (A) illustrated
    (B) accepted
    (C) clarified
    (D) lighted

34. The author implies that most small children believe that the quantity of water changes when it is transferred to a container of a different

    (A) color
    (B) quality
    (C) weight
    (D) shape

35. According to the passage, when small children were asked to count a pile of red and blue pencils they

    (A) counted the number of pencils of each color
    (B) guessed at the total number of pencils
    (C) counted only the pencils of their favorite color
    (D) subtracted the number of red pencils from the number of blue pencils

36. The word "They" in line 17 refers to

    (A) mathematicians
    (B) children
    (C) pencils
    (D) studies

37. The word "prerequisite" in line 19 is closest in meaning to

    (A) reason
    (B) theory
    (C) requirement
    (D) technique

38. The word "itself" in line 20 refers to

    (A) the total
    (B) the concept of abstract numbers
    (C) any class of objects
    (D) setting a table

39. With which of the following statements would the author be LEAST likely to agree?

    (A) Children naturally and easily learn mathematics.
    (B) Children learn to add before they learn to subtract.
    (C) Most people follow the same pattern of mathematical development.
    (D) Mathematical development is subtle and gradual.

40. Where in the passage does the author give an example of a hypothetical experiment?

    (A) Lines 3–6
    (B) Lines 7–9
    (C) Lines 11–14
    (D) Lines 17–20

Questions 41–50

Botany, the study of plants, occupies a peculiar position in the history of human knowledge. For many thousands of years, it was the one field of awareness about which humans had anything more than the vaguest of insights. It is impossible to know today just what our Stone

Line Age ancestors knew about plants, but from what we can observe of preindustrial societies that
(5) still exist, a detailed learning of plants and their properties must be extremely ancient. This is logical. Plants are the basis of the food pyramid for all living things, even for other plants. They have always been enormously important to the welfare of people, not only for food, but also for clothing, weapons, tools, dyes, medicines, shelter, and a great many other purposes. Tribes living today in the jungles of the Amazon recognize literally hundreds of plants and know
(10) many properties of each. To them botany, as such, has no name and is probably not even recognized as a special branch of knowledge at all.

Unfortunately, the more industrialized we become the farther away we move from direct contact with plants, and the less distinct our knowledge of botany grows. Yet everyone comes unconsciously on an amazing amount of botanical knowledge, and few people will fail to
(15) recognize a rose, an apple, or an orchid. When our Neolithic ancestors, living in the Middle East about 10,000 years ago, discovered that certain grasses could be harvested and their seeds planted for richer yields the next season, the first great step in a new association of plants and humans was taken. Grains were discovered and from them flowed the marvel of agriculture: cultivated crops. From then on, humans would increasingly take their living from the controlled
(20) production of a few plants rather than getting a little here and a little there from many varieties that grew wild—and the accumulated knowledge of tens of thousands of years of experience and intimacy with plants in the wild would begin to fade away.

41. Which of the following assumptions about early humans is expressed in the passage?

    (A) They probably had extensive knowledge of plants.
    (B) They divided knowledge into well-defined fields.
    (C) They did not enjoy the study of botany.
    (D) They placed great importance on ownership of property.

42. The word "peculiar" in line 1 is closest in meaning to

    (A) clear
    (B) large
    (C) unusual
    (D) important

43. What does the comment "This is logical" in lines 5–6 mean?

    (A) There is no clear way to determine the extent of our ancestors' knowledge of plants.
    (B) It is not surprising that early humans had a detailed knowledge of plants.
    (C) It is reasonable to assume that our ancestors behaved very much like people in preindustrial societies.
    (D) Human knowledge of plants is well organized and very detailed.

44. The phrase "properties of each" in line 10 refers to each

    (A) tribe
    (B) hundred
    (C) plant
    (D) purpose

45. According to the passage, why has general knowledge of botany declined?

    (A) People no longer value plants as a useful resource.
    (B) Botany is not recognized as a special branch of science.
    (C) Research is unable to keep up with the increasing number of plants.
    (D) Direct contact with a variety of plants has decreased.

46. In line 15, what is the author's purpose in mentioning "a rose, an apple, or an orchid"?

    (A) To make the passage more poetic
    (B) To cite examples of plants that are attractive
    (C) To give botanical examples that most readers will recognize
    (D) To illustrate the diversity of botanical life

47. According to the passage, what was the first great step toward the practice of agriculture?

    (A) The invention of agricultural implements and machinery
    (B) The development of a system of names for plants
    (C) The discovery of grasses that could be harvested and replanted
    (D) The changing diets of early humans

48. The word "controlled" in line 19 is closest in meaning to

    (A) abundant
    (B) managed
    (C) required
    (D) advanced

49. Which of the following can be inferred from the passage about the transition to agriculture?

(A) It forced humans to study plants more carefully so that they would know how to collect and plant seeds.

(B) It led to a more narrow understanding of plants as a source of food, but not for other purposes.

(C) It had a drawback in that humans lost much of their knowledge of wild plants as a result.

(D) It led to a diet that consisted of a greater variety of plants.

50. Where in the passage does the author describe the benefits people derive from plants?

(A) Line 1
(B) Lines 6–8
(C) Lines 10–11
(D) Lines 13–15

THIS IS THE END OF THE QUESTIONS FOR PRACTICE SECTION 3.

Practice Section 3 Review Material

If you have finished the questions in Practice Section 3 and would like to review the Reading Comprehension material, follow these instructions.

Use the answer key below to determine which questions you answered correctly and incorrectly. Then read the following explanations for the correct answers.

Section 3 Answer Key

Passage 1	Passage 2	Passage 3	Passage 4	Passage 5
1. A	11. D	21. A	31. C	41. A
2. D	12. B	22. C	32. A	42. C
3. A	13. C	23. A	33. C	43. B
4. C	14. D	24. A	34. D	44. C
5. C	15. A	25. A	35. A	45. D
6. B	16. D	26. B	36. D	46. C
7. D	17. B	27. B	37. C	47. C
8. D	18. D	28. C	38. B	48. B
9. B	19. C	29. D	39. A	49. C
10. C	20. C	30. A	40. B	50. B

EXPLANATIONS FOR CORRECT ANSWERS

Questions 1–10

1. **(A)** This is the main idea of the passage; each paragraph discusses details about agricultural methods of Native Americans. The other options are topics only discussed in a single paragraph of the passage.

2. **(D)** The verb "solve" in this context is closest in meaning to "deal with." The paragraph goes on to discuss ways of dealing with the water problem, as in possible solutions to the problem.

3. **(A)** Lines 7–8 discuss planting crops in the floodplains and mention flooding. Lines 9–11 go on to explain how building dikes and dams can control flooding and retain water when desired.

4. **(C)** This option is closest in meaning to "enclosing." The sentence talks about building small dikes around stalks of corn.

5. **(C)** Lines 15–16 say "Some crops were planted where they could be watered directly by the runoff from cliff walls." "They" refers to "some crops."

6. **(B)** The answer is found in Lines 17–19, which talk about this strategy. The purpose of planting crops at different places was to ensure that food could be obtained continuously even if one crop failed.

7. **(D)** In this context "same patch of" means the same piece of land. Remember that this word can have other meanings in different contexts.

8. **(D)** The information for answering this question can be found in lines 19–21. The passage contrasts the soil of the woodlands of the eastern United States with the soil elsewhere, which was "not easily exhausted."

9. **(B)** Lines 24–26 mention using local wild plants or going to the mountains to gather wild plants if other food sources failed.

10. **(C)** The passage shows that both having too much rain and too little rain brought problems to agriculture. Therefore, it can be inferred that farmers there would have benefited most from regular rain.

Questions 11–20

11. **(D)** The main focus of the passage is on Marianne Moore's life and work. The other choices are details that are mentioned but not discussed in depth.

12. **(B)** The first paragraph discusses the unusual form of Moore's poems.

13. **(C)** The passage states in lines 3–4 that Moore wrote about animals, laborers, and artists. Fossils are mentioned not as a subject she wrote about but as a metaphor for her style of writing.

14. **(D)** To answer this question correctly you need to understand that Moore is comparing flies trapped in amber to her own collection of quotations from other writers in her poetry. Both the amber and the poetry preserve the original material intact.

15. **(A)** NOTE: By using the word "EXCEPT," the question asks the reader to find which of the choices is not mentioned in the passage. Choices (B), (C), and (D) are mentioned in the second paragraph.

16. **(D)** In this context, the word "period" means "time." A clue to the meaning is in the sentence "During the 1920s she was editor of *The Dial*, an important literary magazine of the period" (lines 12–13).

17. **(B)** The passage states in lines 13–14 that "she lived . . . mostly in Brooklyn." Although Moore did live in the other locations cited, she did not spend "most of her adult life" in any one of them.

18. **(D)** In this context, "succeeding" means "later." Note that it is important to refer back to the passage to choose the correct answer since (A) and (B) can also mean "succeeding" in other contexts.

19. **(C)** In this sentence, "it" refers to the necessity of earning a living (lines 20–21).

20. **(C)** The idea that Moore wrote because she wanted to express herself is stated in lines 21–22.

Questions 21–30

21. **(A)** In this context, "suggest" means "imply." Lines 6–9 discuss the connection between the name "eel-form" and its meaning.

22. **(C)** In this sentence, the pronoun "it" refers to "body." The sentences discusses the motion an eel uses to push its body through the water.

23. **(A)** In lines 10–12 the author tells us that "Eel-form swimming is effective but not particularly efficient because the undulations increase the drag, or resistance in the water."

24. **(A)** In this sentence the word "employed" means that this swimming style is "used" primarily by bottom dwellers. Therefore, "used" is the best answer.

25. **(A)** You do not have to know what blennies are to answer this question. Lines 13–14 say that blennies swim in the same way as eels, while lines 12–13 say that this swimming style is used mainly by "bottom dwellers." This implies that blennies are bottom dwellers.

26. **(B)** Since the sentence goes on to say that this type of body feature "helps keep the body still," we can see that the word "minimizes" means "reduces."

27. **(B)** Paragraph 3 discusses characteristics of "jack-form swimming." You can find the answer in lines 25–26, which say "Jack-form fish are efficient swimmers, as they must be to catch their prey."

28. **(C)** In this context, the word "objective" means "purpose."

29. **(D)** This question requires you to identify where the specific information is stated in the passage. Lines 30–32 tell us that the fish that are poisonous are "puffer fish."

30. **(A)** Use the process of elimination to identify the option that can be supported by the passage content. (B), (C), and (D) are all contradicted in the passage, so choose the first option, (A).

Questions 31–40

31. **(C)** While all of the answer choices make some reference to mathematics, the development of math ability in children is the main topic. The idea of development occurs throughout the passage.

32. **(A)** The sentence that begins "Not long after learning to walk and talk, they can set the table with impressive accuracy" (lines 3–4) provides information about when children learn simple counting.

33. **(C)** Note that it is important to refer to the passage to select the correct answer, since (D) can also mean "illuminated" in another context.

34. **(D)** The answer can be deduced from the information in line 14. "Short stout" and "tall thin" refer to the shapes of containers.

35. **(A)** The correct answer is stated in lines 15–16: "children . . . readily report the number of blue or red pencils."

36. **(D)** "They" refers to the subject of the previous sentence, "Such studies" (line 16).

37. **(C)** A prerequisite is something that is required, or needed, before some other thing is possible. In this situation, you must know the meaning of the word being tested; context alone is not sufficient.

38. **(B)** The word "itself" refers to the noun phrase that precedes the parenthetical information that is set off by dashes. The dashes indicate extra information that is considered as separate from the main part of the sentence.

39. **(A)** NOTE: By using the word "LEAST," the question asks the reader to decide which of the statements contradicts the information given in the passage. Review the passage to check how the information in each of the choices is presented in the passage.

40. **(B)** You should read the specific lines indicated to find which ones contain the information asked for in the question. In this case, the subjunctive form, "if a child were secluded," is used to state a hypothetical, not real, situation.

Questions 41–50

41. **(A)** Throughout the passage the author stresses the fact that people have known a lot about plants for a very long time. See lines 2–3, 5–6, 8–10, 14, 15, and 18–20.

42. **(C)** In this context, "peculiar" means "unusual." There is a clue to this meaning in the statement that "botany. . . was the one field of awareness about which humans had anything more than the vaguest of insights" (lines 1–3). This means that people knew a lot about plants, probably more than they knew about other areas.

43. **(B)** "This is logical" refers to the preceding information, which states that humans had a lot of detailed knowledge about plants because plants were important to them.

44. **(C)** This phrase refers to each plant, since "plants" is the only logical referent.

45. **(D)** The passage states in lines 12–13 that "the more industrialized we become . . . the less distinct our knowledge of botany grows." This means that people now have less direct contact with plants than they had previously. The same idea is also stated in lines 19–22.

46. **(C)** Roses, apples, and orchids are common plants with which most people are familiar.

47. **(C)** The answer to this question is directly stated in lines 16–17.

48. **(B)** "Managed" is the answer because it is the only choice that means "controlled."

49. **(C)** The passage states in lines 21–22 that "the accumulated knowledge of tens of thousands of years . . . would begin to fade away." It can be inferred that this loss of knowledge was not a positive development.

50. **(B)** You should read the specific lines indicated to find which contain the information asked for in the question. The benefits people derive from plants are presented in lines 6–8.

CHAPTER 6

Complete *TOEFL ITP* Practice Test

General Directions

This is a test of your ability to understand and use the English language. The test is divided into three sections, and each section or part of a section begins with a set of specific directions. The directions include sample questions. Before you begin to work on a section or part, be sure that you understand what you will need to do.

The supervisor will tell you when to start each section and when to stop and go on to the next section. You should work quickly but carefully. Do not spend too much time on any one question. If you finish a section early, you may review your answers **on that section only**. You may **not** go on to a new section, and you may **not** return to a section that you have already left.

You will find that some of the questions are more difficult than others, but you should try to answer every one. Your score will be based on the number of **correct** answers you give. If you are not sure of the correct answer to a question, make the best guess you can. It is to your advantage to answer every question, even if you have to guess the answer.

Do not mark your answers in the test book. **You must mark all of your answers on the separate answer sheet** that the supervisor will give to you. When you mark your answer to a question on your answer sheet, you must:

- Use a medium-soft (#2 or HB) black lead pencil.
- Check the number of the question, and find that number on your answer sheet. Then, after that number, find the oval with the letter of the answer you have chosen.
- Carefully make a dark mark that completely fills the oval so that you cannot see the letter inside the oval.
- Mark **only one** answer to each question.
- Erase all extra marks completely. If you change your mind about an answer after you have marked it on your answer sheet, erase your old answer completely, and mark your new answer.
- After the supervisor tells you to stop your work, you will not be permitted to make any additional corrections.

The examples below show you the **correct** way and **wrong** ways of marking an answer sheet.

Be sure to fill in the ovals on your answer sheet the **correct** way.

Use the answer sheet on the next page to record your answers for all three sections of the Complete Test.

SECTION 1

1 (A)(B)(C)(D)	21 (A)(B)(C)(D)	41 (A)(B)(C)(D)
2 (A)(B)(C)(D)	22 (A)(B)(C)(D)	42 (A)(B)(C)(D)
3 (A)(B)(C)(D)	23 (A)(B)(C)(D)	43 (A)(B)(C)(D)
4 (A)(B)(C)(D)	24 (A)(B)(C)(D)	44 (A)(B)(C)(D)
5 (A)(B)(C)(D)	25 (A)(B)(C)(D)	45 (A)(B)(C)(D)
6 (A)(B)(C)(D)	26 (A)(B)(C)(D)	46 (A)(B)(C)(D)
7 (A)(B)(C)(D)	27 (A)(B)(C)(D)	47 (A)(B)(C)(D)
8 (A)(B)(C)(D)	28 (A)(B)(C)(D)	48 (A)(B)(C)(D)
9 (A)(B)(C)(D)	29 (A)(B)(C)(D)	49 (A)(B)(C)(D)
10 (A)(B)(C)(D)	30 (A)(B)(C)(D)	50 (A)(B)(C)(D)
11 (A)(B)(C)(D)	31 (A)(B)(C)(D)	
12 (A)(B)(C)(D)	32 (A)(B)(C)(D)	
13 (A)(B)(C)(D)	33 (A)(B)(C)(D)	
14 (A)(B)(C)(D)	34 (A)(B)(C)(D)	
15 (A)(B)(C)(D)	35 (A)(B)(C)(D)	
16 (A)(B)(C)(D)	36 (A)(B)(C)(D)	
17 (A)(B)(C)(D)	37 (A)(B)(C)(D)	
18 (A)(B)(C)(D)	38 (A)(B)(C)(D)	
19 (A)(B)(C)(D)	39 (A)(B)(C)(D)	
20 (A)(B)(C)(D)	40 (A)(B)(C)(D)	

SECTION 2

1 (A)(B)(C)(D)	21 (A)(B)(C)(D)
2 (A)(B)(C)(D)	22 (A)(B)(C)(D)
3 (A)(B)(C)(D)	23 (A)(B)(C)(D)
4 (A)(B)(C)(D)	24 (A)(B)(C)(D)
5 (A)(B)(C)(D)	25 (A)(B)(C)(D)
6 (A)(B)(C)(D)	26 (A)(B)(C)(D)
7 (A)(B)(C)(D)	27 (A)(B)(C)(D)
8 (A)(B)(C)(D)	28 (A)(B)(C)(D)
9 (A)(B)(C)(D)	29 (A)(B)(C)(D)
10 (A)(B)(C)(D)	30 (A)(B)(C)(D)
11 (A)(B)(C)(D)	31 (A)(B)(C)(D)
12 (A)(B)(C)(D)	32 (A)(B)(C)(D)
13 (A)(B)(C)(D)	33 (A)(B)(C)(D)
14 (A)(B)(C)(D)	34 (A)(B)(C)(D)
15 (A)(B)(C)(D)	35 (A)(B)(C)(D)
16 (A)(B)(C)(D)	36 (A)(B)(C)(D)
17 (A)(B)(C)(D)	37 (A)(B)(C)(D)
18 (A)(B)(C)(D)	38 (A)(B)(C)(D)
19 (A)(B)(C)(D)	39 (A)(B)(C)(D)
20 (A)(B)(C)(D)	40 (A)(B)(C)(D)

SECTION 3

1 (A)(B)(C)(D)	21 (A)(B)(C)(D)	41 (A)(B)(C)(D)
2 (A)(B)(C)(D)	22 (A)(B)(C)(D)	42 (A)(B)(C)(D)
3 (A)(B)(C)(D)	23 (A)(B)(C)(D)	43 (A)(B)(C)(D)
4 (A)(B)(C)(D)	24 (A)(B)(C)(D)	44 (A)(B)(C)(D)
5 (A)(B)(C)(D)	25 (A)(B)(C)(D)	45 (A)(B)(C)(D)
6 (A)(B)(C)(D)	26 (A)(B)(C)(D)	46 (A)(B)(C)(D)
7 (A)(B)(C)(D)	27 (A)(B)(C)(D)	47 (A)(B)(C)(D)
8 (A)(B)(C)(D)	28 (A)(B)(C)(D)	48 (A)(B)(C)(D)
9 (A)(B)(C)(D)	29 (A)(B)(C)(D)	49 (A)(B)(C)(D)
10 (A)(B)(C)(D)	30 (A)(B)(C)(D)	50 (A)(B)(C)(D)
11 (A)(B)(C)(D)	31 (A)(B)(C)(D)	
12 (A)(B)(C)(D)	32 (A)(B)(C)(D)	
13 (A)(B)(C)(D)	33 (A)(B)(C)(D)	
14 (A)(B)(C)(D)	34 (A)(B)(C)(D)	
15 (A)(B)(C)(D)	35 (A)(B)(C)(D)	
16 (A)(B)(C)(D)	36 (A)(B)(C)(D)	
17 (A)(B)(C)(D)	37 (A)(B)(C)(D)	
18 (A)(B)(C)(D)	38 (A)(B)(C)(D)	
19 (A)(B)(C)(D)	39 (A)(B)(C)(D)	
20 (A)(B)(C)(D)	40 (A)(B)(C)(D)	

SECTION 1

1 (A)(B)(C)(D)	21 (A)(B)(C)(D)	41 (A)(B)(C)(D)
2 (A)(B)(C)(D)	22 (A)(B)(C)(D)	42 (A)(B)(C)(D)
3 (A)(B)(C)(D)	23 (A)(B)(C)(D)	43 (A)(B)(C)(D)
4 (A)(B)(C)(D)	24 (A)(B)(C)(D)	44 (A)(B)(C)(D)
5 (A)(B)(C)(D)	25 (A)(B)(C)(D)	45 (A)(B)(C)(D)
6 (A)(B)(C)(D)	26 (A)(B)(C)(D)	46 (A)(B)(C)(D)
7 (A)(B)(C)(D)	27 (A)(B)(C)(D)	47 (A)(B)(C)(D)
8 (A)(B)(C)(D)	28 (A)(B)(C)(D)	48 (A)(B)(C)(D)
9 (A)(B)(C)(D)	29 (A)(B)(C)(D)	49 (A)(B)(C)(D)
10 (A)(B)(C)(D)	30 (A)(B)(C)(D)	50 (A)(B)(C)(D)
11 (A)(B)(C)(D)	31 (A)(B)(C)(D)	
12 (A)(B)(C)(D)	32 (A)(B)(C)(D)	
13 (A)(B)(C)(D)	33 (A)(B)(C)(D)	
14 (A)(B)(C)(D)	34 (A)(B)(C)(D)	
15 (A)(B)(C)(D)	35 (A)(B)(C)(D)	
16 (A)(B)(C)(D)	36 (A)(B)(C)(D)	
17 (A)(B)(C)(D)	37 (A)(B)(C)(D)	
18 (A)(B)(C)(D)	38 (A)(B)(C)(D)	
19 (A)(B)(C)(D)	39 (A)(B)(C)(D)	
20 (A)(B)(C)(D)	40 (A)(B)(C)(D)	

SECTION 2

1 (A)(B)(C)(D)	21 (A)(B)(C)(D)
2 (A)(B)(C)(D)	22 (A)(B)(C)(D)
3 (A)(B)(C)(D)	23 (A)(B)(C)(D)
4 (A)(B)(C)(D)	24 (A)(B)(C)(D)
5 (A)(B)(C)(D)	25 (A)(B)(C)(D)
6 (A)(B)(C)(D)	26 (A)(B)(C)(D)
7 (A)(B)(C)(D)	27 (A)(B)(C)(D)
8 (A)(B)(C)(D)	28 (A)(B)(C)(D)
9 (A)(B)(C)(D)	29 (A)(B)(C)(D)
10 (A)(B)(C)(D)	30 (A)(B)(C)(D)
11 (A)(B)(C)(D)	31 (A)(B)(C)(D)
12 (A)(B)(C)(D)	32 (A)(B)(C)(D)
13 (A)(B)(C)(D)	33 (A)(B)(C)(D)
14 (A)(B)(C)(D)	34 (A)(B)(C)(D)
15 (A)(B)(C)(D)	35 (A)(B)(C)(D)
16 (A)(B)(C)(D)	36 (A)(B)(C)(D)
17 (A)(B)(C)(D)	37 (A)(B)(C)(D)
18 (A)(B)(C)(D)	38 (A)(B)(C)(D)
19 (A)(B)(C)(D)	39 (A)(B)(C)(D)
20 (A)(B)(C)(D)	40 (A)(B)(C)(D)

SECTION 3

1 (A)(B)(C)(D)	21 (A)(B)(C)(D)	41 (A)(B)(C)(D)
2 (A)(B)(C)(D)	22 (A)(B)(C)(D)	42 (A)(B)(C)(D)
3 (A)(B)(C)(D)	23 (A)(B)(C)(D)	43 (A)(B)(C)(D)
4 (A)(B)(C)(D)	24 (A)(B)(C)(D)	44 (A)(B)(C)(D)
5 (A)(B)(C)(D)	25 (A)(B)(C)(D)	45 (A)(B)(C)(D)
6 (A)(B)(C)(D)	26 (A)(B)(C)(D)	46 (A)(B)(C)(D)
7 (A)(B)(C)(D)	27 (A)(B)(C)(D)	47 (A)(B)(C)(D)
8 (A)(B)(C)(D)	28 (A)(B)(C)(D)	48 (A)(B)(C)(D)
9 (A)(B)(C)(D)	29 (A)(B)(C)(D)	49 (A)(B)(C)(D)
10 (A)(B)(C)(D)	30 (A)(B)(C)(D)	50 (A)(B)(C)(D)
11 (A)(B)(C)(D)	31 (A)(B)(C)(D)	
12 (A)(B)(C)(D)	32 (A)(B)(C)(D)	
13 (A)(B)(C)(D)	33 (A)(B)(C)(D)	
14 (A)(B)(C)(D)	34 (A)(B)(C)(D)	
15 (A)(B)(C)(D)	35 (A)(B)(C)(D)	
16 (A)(B)(C)(D)	36 (A)(B)(C)(D)	
17 (A)(B)(C)(D)	37 (A)(B)(C)(D)	
18 (A)(B)(C)(D)	38 (A)(B)(C)(D)	
19 (A)(B)(C)(D)	39 (A)(B)(C)(D)	
20 (A)(B)(C)(D)	40 (A)(B)(C)(D)	

Section 1

Listening Comprehension

Now set your audio player to Track 5.

In this section of the test, you will have an opportunity to demonstrate your ability to understand conversations and talks in English. There are three parts to this section with special directions for each part. Answer all the questions on the basis of what is stated or implied by the speaker in this test. Do not take notes or write in your test book at any time. Do not turn the pages until you are told to do so.

Part A

Directions: In Part A, you will hear short conversations between two people. After each conversation, you will hear a question about the conversation. The conversations and questions will not be repeated.

After you hear a question, read the four possible answers in your test book and choose the best answer. Then, on your answer sheet, find the number of the question and fill in the space that corresponds to the letter of the answer you have chosen.

Here is an example.

On your recording, you hear:

Sample Answer
● Ⓑ Ⓒ Ⓓ

In your test book, you read:

    (A) He does not like the painting either.
    (B) He does not know how to paint.
    (C) He does not have any paintings.
    (D) He does not know what to do.

You learn from the conversation that neither the man nor the woman likes the painting. The best answer to the question "What does the man mean?" is (A), "He does not like the painting either." Therefore, the correct choice is (A).

1. (A) Go to the movies with the man
   (B) Take her brother to the movies
   (C) Eat at her brother's home
   (D) Cook dinner with Lois

2. (A) The man should have offered his assistance earlier.
   (B) She does not need the man's help.
   (C) She did not realize the boxes were empty.
   (D) She wants the man to move the boxes.

3. (A) He would like to have the windows open.
   (B) He rarely leaves the windows open.
   (C) He thinks the air is polluted.
   (D) He will help her close the windows.

4. (A) The results might be ready tomorrow.
   (B) The man needs another test tomorrow.
   (C) The results were called in last night.
   (D) The doctor called the lab again.

5. (A) She does not remember much about Portland.
   (B) She has never been to Portland.
   (C) She knows someone else who could help him.
   (D) She would be happy to talk to the man later.

6. (A) Turn down the volume
   (B) Help the man study for a test
   (C) Play a different kind of music
   (D) Speak louder

7. (A) She forgot when the report was due.
   (B) She would like the man to help her with the report.
   (C) She needs more time to finish the report.
   (D) She has not included any data in her report.

8. (A) The cat is causing him problems.
   (B) The cat is quite friendly.
   (C) He does not get along with Debbie.
   (D) He is glad Debbie gave him the cat.

9. (A) Try to get a seat next to the window
   (B) Find another passenger going to Cleveland
   (C) Ask for information about the departure time
   (D) Find out if there are any seats left on the bus

10. (A) She forgot to stop at the store.
    (B) The man should not eat the fish.
    (C) The fish is safe to eat.
    (D) The food should not be reheated.

Go on to the next page

11. (A) She will not be able to go with the man.
    (B) She does not think Frank is arriving until tomorrow morning.
    (C) She has to pick up Frank at 2:00.
    (D) She does not know when her class will end.

12. (A) He watched the television program with his mother.
    (B) His mother reminded him that his professor was on television.
    (C) Answering the phone caused him to miss the television program.
    (D) His mother missed the television program.

13. (A) The pool will be open all week.
    (B) The weather will cool down soon.
    (C) The woman should go swimming.
    (D) He prefers to stay inside in hot weather.

14. (A) He may not have enough time to cook.
    (B) He may spend more money on food next semester.
    (C) He may gain weight if he does his own cooking.
    (D) He may not enjoy cooking.

15. (A) He is tired.
    (B) He lost the race.
    (C) He has already been to the top of the hill.
    (D) He prefers doing exercise indoors.

16. (A) The doctor only has time on Tuesdays.
    (B) The doctor is busy on Tuesday morning.
    (C) The man must come more than one time.
    (D) The man must arrive on time.

17. (A) Eat at the cafeteria more often
    (B) Find out when the cafeteria opens
    (C) Meet her in the cafeteria this evening
    (D) Try to get a job at the cafeteria

18. (A) Cancel their trip
    (B) Make a quick stop for a meal
    (C) Arrive at their destination early
    (D) Have a longer lunch than originally planned

19. (A) She does not want to take the course this semester.
    (B) She thought the class would be easy.
    (C) She is surprised that all the sections are filled.
    (D) There are only thirteen students in the psychology class.

20. (A) He does not like to drink coffee.
    (B) He is not upset by the accident.
    (C) The woman should apologize.
    (D) The woman has spilled coffee on him before.

Go on to the next page ➡

Complete *TOEFL ITP* Practice Test   105

21. (A) The woman will have to buy a new sweater.
    (B) The sweater looks just like the woman's new one.
    (C) The sweater can be repaired easily.
    (D) The woman should not put sharp objects in her sweater pocket.

22. (A) The jackets sold out quickly.
    (B) The sale ended yesterday.
    (C) He will check with the sales clerk.
    (D) The woman might find a jacket on sale.

23. (A) She likes to drive when she travels.
    (B) She does not want to go to Chicago.
    (C) She does not know how much the train trip will cost.
    (D) It is cheaper to go to Chicago by car.

24. (A) The man paid a lot to join the gym.
    (B) The man has been working too hard.
    (C) The man has improved his physical appearance.
    (D) The man should find a better job.

25. (A) She prefers hot weather.
    (B) The man should visit Washington when it is cooler.
    (C) She agrees that going to the beach would have been better.
    (D) Visiting Washington is enjoyable despite the heat.

26. (A) She will help the man clean up the lounge.
    (B) The mother should be more considerate.
    (C) The man should be more understanding.
    (D) The child is not well behaved for his age.

27. (A) He can meet the woman on Wednesday.
    (B) He will not be ready until next week.
    (C) He is available any day except Wednesday.
    (D) He needs to do the history project before Wednesday.

28. (A) Prepare for an important game
    (B) Try out for the field hockey team
    (C) Get tickets to see the championship game
    (D) Receive an award for winning a championship

29. (A) She wants to check the weather before deciding.
    (B) She has a problem with her hearing.
    (C) She would enjoy having dinner another time.
    (D) She wants the man to help her with some work.

30. (A) The back of the drawer has fallen off.
    (B) The man does not have any soap.
    (C) The cabinet is too heavy to move.
    (D) Something is blocking the back of the drawer.

Go on to the next page ➤

Part B

Directions: In this part of the test, you will hear longer conversations. After each conversation, you will hear several questions. The conversations and questions will not be repeated.

After you hear a question, read the four possible answers in your test book and choose the best answer. Then, on your answer sheet, find the number of the question and fill in the space that corresponds to the letter of the answer you have chosen.

Remember, you are not allowed to take notes or write in your test book.

31. (A) They lived in caves.
    (B) They traveled in groups.
    (C) They had an advanced language.
    (D) They ate mostly fruit.

32. (A) It was unavailable because dry
        weather had killed the trees.
    (B) It was used to build shelters in
        some regions.
    (C) It was used mainly for heating
        and cooking.
    (D) Ice Age people did not have the
        tools to work with wood.

33. (A) They wore clothing made of
        animal skins.
    (B) They used sand as insulation.
    (C) They kept fires burning constantly.
    (D) They faced their homes toward
        the south.

34. (A) Meet his anthropology teacher
    (B) Lend him her magazine when she
        is done with it
    (C) Help him with an assignment
        about the Ice Age
    (D) Help him study for an
        anthropology test

35. (A) Mating habits of squid and
        octopus
    (B) The evolution of certain forms
        of sea life
    (C) The study of marine shells
    (D) Survival skills of sea creatures

36. (A) He did not understand the lecture.
    (B) He wants to borrow her notes
        next week.
    (C) He needs help preparing for
        an exam.
    (D) He was sick and unable to attend
        the lecture.

37. (A) Some sea creatures developed
        vertebrae.
    (B) The first giant squid was captured.
    (C) Some sea creatures shed their
        shells.
    (D) Sea life became more intelligent.

38. (A) She has always believed they
        exist.
    (B) She heard about them in New
        Zealand.
    (C) Stories about them may be based
        on giant squid.
    (D) The instructor mentioned them
        in the lecture.

Go on to the next page

Part C

Directions: In this part of the test, you will hear several short talks. After each talk, you will hear some questions. The talks and the questions will not be repeated.

After you hear a question, read the four possible answers in your test book and choose the best answer. Then, on your answer sheet, find the number of the question and fill in the space that corresponds to the letter of the answer you have chosen.

Here is an example.

On the recording, you hear:

Now listen to a sample question.

In your test book, you read:

   (A) To demonstrate the latest use of computer graphics
   (B) To discuss the possibility of an economic depression
   (C) To explain the workings of the brain
   (D) To dramatize a famous mystery story

The best answer to the question "What is the main purpose of the program?" is (C), "To explain the workings of the brain." Therefore, the correct choice is (C).

Now listen to another sample question.

In your test book, you read:

   (A) It is required of all science majors.
   (B) It will never be shown again.
   (C) It can help viewers improve their memory skills.
   (D) It will help with course work.

The best answer to the question "Why does the speaker recommend watching the program?" is (D), "It will help with course work." Therefore, the correct choice is (D).

Remember, you are **not** allowed to take notes or write in your test book.

39. (A) That babies understand language before they can speak
    (B) That babies have simple mathematical skills
    (C) That babies prefer different kinds of toys
    (D) That television has a strong influence on babies

40. (A) Staring at the dolls longer
    (B) Crying loudly
    (C) Blinking their eyes rapidly
    (D) Reaching for the dolls

41. (A) They are born with the ability to count.
    (B) They are exceptionally intelligent.
    (C) They learned to count from playing with dolls.
    (D) They have learned to count from their parents.

42. (A) Language ability might be negatively affected.
    (B) Babies who learn quickly might develop learning problems later.
    (C) Parents might try to teach their children certain skills at too early an age.
    (D) Learning math early might interfere with creativity.

43. (A) To review what students know about volcanic activity
    (B) To demonstrate the use of a new measurement device
    (C) To explain the answer to an examination question
    (D) To provide background for the next reading assignment

44. (A) They occur at regular intervals.
    (B) They can withstand great heat.
    (C) They travel through Earth's interior.
    (D) They can record Earth's internal temperature.

45. (A) When Earth was formed
    (B) The composition of the Earth's interior
    (C) Why lava is hot
    (D) How often a volcano is likely to erupt

46. (A) How deep they are
    (B) Where earthquakes form
    (C) How hot they are
    (D) What purpose they serve

47. (A) Photographic techniques common in the early 1900s
    (B) The early life of Alfred Stieglitz
    (C) The influence of weather on Alfred Stieglitz' photography
    (D) Alfred Stieglitz' approach to photography

48. (A) How to analyze photographic techniques
    (B) How to classify photography
    (C) How Alfred Stieglitz contributed to the history of photography
    (D) Whether photography is superior to other art forms

49. (A) They were influenced by his background in engineering.
    (B) They were very expensive to take.
    (C) They were among the first taken under such conditions.
    (D) Most of them were of poor quality.

50. (A) He thought that the copying process took too long.
    (B) He considered each photograph to be an individual work of art.
    (C) He did not have the necessary equipment for reproduction.
    (D) He did not want them to be displayed outside of his home.

THIS IS THE END OF SECTION 1.
STOP WORK ON SECTION 1.
TURN OFF YOUR AUDIO PLAYER.

Section 2

Structure and Written Expression

Time: 25 minutes

Now set your clock for 25 minutes.

This section is designed to measure your ability to recognize language that is appropriate for standard written English. There are two types of questions in this section, with special directions for each type.

STRUCTURE

Directions: Questions 1–15 are incomplete sentences. Beneath each sentence you will see four words or phrases, marked (A), (B), (C), and (D). Choose the one word or phrase that best completes the sentence. Then, on your answer sheet, find the number of the question and fill in the space that corresponds to the letter of the answer you have chosen.

Example I

Sample Answer

Ⓐ ● Ⓒ Ⓓ

Geysers have often been compared to volcanoes ------- both emit hot liquids from below Earth's surface.

    (A) despite
    (B) because
    (C) in regard to
    (D) as a result of

The sentence should read: "Geysers have often been compared to volcanoes because both emit hot liquids from below Earth's surface." Therefore, you should choose (B).

Example II

Sample Answer

Ⓐ Ⓑ Ⓒ ●

During the early period of ocean navigation, ------- any need for sophisticated instruments and techniques.

    (A) so that hardly
    (B) when there hardly was
    (C) hardly was
    (D) there was hardly

The sentence should read: "During the early period of ocean navigation, there was hardly any need for sophisticated instruments and techniques." Therefore, you should choose (D).

NOW BEGIN WORK ON THE QUESTIONS.

1. Tourism is ------- leading source of income for many coastal communities.

   (A) a
   (B) at
   (C) then
   (D) none

2. Although thunder and lightning are produced at the same time, light waves travel faster -------, so we see the lightning before we hear the thunder.

   (A) than sound waves do
   (B) than sound waves are
   (C) do sound waves
   (D) sound waves

3. Beef cattle ------- of all livestock for economic growth in the North American economy.

   (A) the most are important
   (B) are the most important
   (C) the most important are
   (D) that are the most important

4. The discovery of the halftone process in photography in 1881 made it ------- photographs in books and newspapers.

   (A) the possible reproduction
   (B) possible to reproduce
   (C) the possibility of reproducing
   (D) possibly reproduced

5. Flag Day is a legal holiday only in the state of Pennsylvania, -------, according to tradition, Betsy Ross sewed the first American flag.

   (A) which
   (B) where
   (C) that
   (D) has

6. ------- vastness of the Grand Canyon, it is difficult to capture it in a single photograph.

   (A) While the
   (B) The
   (C) For the
   (D) Because of the

7. Speciation, -------, results when an animal population becomes isolated by some factor, usually geographic.

   (A) form biological species
   (B) biological species are formed
   (C) which forming biological species
   (D) the formation of biological species

8. In its pure state antimony has no important uses, but ------- with other substances, it is an extremely useful metal.

   (A) when combined physically or chemically
   (B) combined when physically or chemically
   (C) the physical and chemical combination
   (D) it is combined physically and chemically

9. The dawn redwood appears
   ------- some 100 million years ago in
   northern forests around the world.

   (A) was flourished
   (B) having to flourish
   (C) to have flourished
   (D) have flourished

10. Beginning in the Middle Ages,
    composers of Western music used a
    system of notating their compositions
    ------- be performed by musicians.

    (A) will
    (B) that
    (C) and when to
    (D) so they could

11. Civil rights are the freedoms and
    rights ------- as a member of a
    community, state, or nation.

    (A) may have a person
    (B) may have a person who
    (C) a person may have
    (D) and a person may have

12. Richard Wright enjoyed success
    and influence ------- among Black
    American writers of his era.

    (A) were unparalleled
    (B) are unparalleled
    (C) unparalleled
    (D) the unparalleled

13. ------- of large mammals once
    dominated the North American
    prairies: the American bison and the
    pronghorn antelope.

    (A) There are two species
    (B) With two species
    (C) Two species are
    (D) Two species

14. Franklin D. Roosevelt was
    ------- the great force of radio and the
    opportunity it provided for taking
    government policies directly to the
    people.

    (A) as the first president he
        understood fully

    (B) the first President that, to fully
        understand

    (C) the first President fully
        understood

    (D) the first President to understand
        fully

15. During the late fifteenth century,
    ------- of the native societies of
    America had professions in the fields
    of arts and crafts.

    (A) only a few
    (B) a few but
    (C) few, but only
    (D) a few only

WRITTEN EXPRESSION

Directions: In questions 16–40, each sentence has four underlined words or phrases. The four underlined parts of the sentence are marked (A), (B), (C), and (D). Choose the one underlined word or phrase that must be changed for the sentence to be correct. Then, on your answer sheet, find the number of the question and fill in the space that corresponds to the letter of the answer you have chosen.

Example I

Guppies are sometimes <u>call</u> rainbow <u>fish</u> <u>due to</u> the <u>bright</u> colors of the males.
                    A   B   C   D

The sentence should read: "Guppies are sometimes called rainbow fish due to the bright colors of the males." Therefore, you should choose (A).

Example II

<u>Serving</u> several <u>term</u> in the United States Congress, Shirley Chisholm became a <u>respected</u>
  A   B   C
United States <u>politician</u>.
                 D

The sentence should read: "Serving several terms in the United States Congress, Shirley Chisholm became a respected United States politician" Therefore, you should choose (B).

NOW BEGIN WORK ON THE QUESTIONS.

16. Jane Addams, social worker, author, and <u>spokeswoman</u> for the peace and women's
                                              A
    suffrage <u>movements, she received</u> the Nobel Peace Prize in 1931 for her <u>humanitarian</u>
            B   C   D
    achievements.

17. The <u>public ceremonies</u> of the North American Plains Indians are <u>lesser</u> elaborate
           A   B
    <u>than those</u> of the Navajo <u>in</u> the Southwest.
        C   D

18. In <u>some</u> species of fish, <u>such the</u> three-spined stickleback, the male, not the female,
        A   B
    <u>performs</u> the task of <u>caring</u> for the young.
        C   D

19. When she <u>retires</u> in September 1989, <u>tennis champion</u> Christine Evert was <u>the most</u>
              A   B   C
    famous <u>woman athlete</u> in the United States.
            D

20. <u>The</u> ancient Romans used vessels <u>equipped</u> with sails <u>and</u> banks of oars <u>to transporting</u>
     A   B   C   D
    their armies.

21. Dinosaurs <u>are</u> traditionally classified as cold-blooded reptiles, <u>but</u> recent evidence
              A   B
    based on eating habits, posture, and skeletal <u>structural</u> suggests some <u>may have been</u>
                                                   C   D
    warm-blooded.

22. Since the Great Depression of the 1930s, government <u>programs</u> such as Social
                                                         A
    Security have <u>been built</u> into the economy <u>to help</u> avert <u>severity</u> business declines.
                   B   C   D

23. In the 1970s, <u>consumer</u> activists <u>succeeded in</u> promoting laws that set <u>safety</u> standards
                   A   B   C
    for automobiles, children's clothing, and a <u>widely</u> range of household products.
                                                 D

24. Zoos in New Orleans, San Diego, Detroit, and the Bronx <u>have become</u> biological
                                                            A
    parks <u>where</u> animals <u>roams freely</u> and people <u>watch from</u> across a moat.
           B   C   D

25. In primates, as in other <u>mammal</u>, hairs <u>around</u> the eyes and ears and in the nose,
                                 A   B

    <u>prevent</u> dust, insects, and other matter from <u>entering</u> these organs.
       C   D

26. The Rocky Mountains <u>were</u> explored <u>by</u> fur traders during the early 1800s, in <u>a</u>
                            A   B   C

    decades <u>preceding</u> the United States Civil War.
           D

27. The works of the <u>author</u> Herman Melville are <u>literary</u> creations of a high order,
                   A   B

    blending <u>fact</u>, fiction, adventure, and subtle <u>symbolic</u>.
           C   D

28. <u>Each chemical</u> element is characterized <u>to</u> the number of protons that <u>an atom</u> of that
            A   B   C

    element contains, called <u>its</u> atomic number.
                         D

29. The <u>body structure</u> that developed in birds <u>over</u> millions of years is <u>well designed</u> for
              A   B   C

    flight, being both <u>lightly</u> in weight and remarkably strong.
                  D

30. <u>From</u> 1905 to 1920, American novelist Edith Wharton <u>was</u> at the height of her
     A   B

    writing career, producing <u>of her</u> three <u>most</u> popular novels.
                            C   D

31. In the early twentieth century, there was considerable <u>interesting</u> among sociologists
                                                       A

    in the fact <u>that</u> in the United States <u>the family</u> was losing its <u>traditional</u> roles.
             B   C   D

32. <u>Although</u> diamond is colorless and transparent <u>when</u> pure, <u>it</u> may appear in various
       A   B   C

    <u>color</u>, ranging from pastels to opaque black, if it is contaminated with other material.
     D

33. Comparative anatomy is <u>concerned to</u> the <u>structural</u> differences <u>among</u> animal <u>forms</u>.
                                A   B   C   D

34. A seismograph records oscillation of the ground <u>caused by</u> seismic waves, vibrations
                                              A

    that <u>travel</u> from <u>its</u> point of origin <u>through</u> Earth or along its surface.
        B   C   D

35. Electric lamps came into widespread use during the early 1900s and eventually <u>replaced</u> once-popular <u>type</u> of fat, gas, or <u>oil</u> lamps for <u>almost every</u> purpose.
     A   B   C   D

36. Located in Canada, the Columbia Icefield <u>covers area</u> of 120 square miles <u>and</u> is
                                               A   B

    3,300 feet <u>thick</u> in some <u>places</u>.
              C   D

37. Composer Richard Rodgers and lyricist Oscar Hammerstein II <u>brought</u> to the musical
                                                           A

    Oklahoma! <u>extensive</u> musical and theatrical backgrounds as well as <u>familiar</u> with the
                   B   C

    <u>traditional</u> forms of operetta and musical comedy.
        D

38. Although traditional flutes are <u>among</u> the world's oldest musical instruments, <u>but the</u>
                               A   B

    flute <u>used</u> in orchestras today is <u>one of</u> the most technically sophisticated.
          C   D

39. Rice, <u>which it still</u> forms the staple diet of <u>much</u> of the world's population, grows
                   A   B

    <u>best</u> in <u>hot</u>, wet lands.
      C   D

40. Federal funds appropriated <u>for art</u> in the 1930s made possible <u>hundreds of</u> murals and
                                A   B

    statues still <u>admiration</u> in small towns <u>all over</u> the United States.
             C   D

THIS IS THE END OF THE STRUCTURE AND WRITTEN EXPRESSION SECTION.

IF YOU FINISH IN LESS THAN 25 MINUTES, CHECK YOUR WORK IN SECTION 2 ONLY.

DO NOT READ OR WORK ON ANY OTHER SECTION OF THE TEST.

AT THE END OF 25 MINUTES, GO ON TO SECTION 3—READING COMPREHENSION. USE EXACTLY 55 MINUTES TO WORK ON SECTION 3.

Section 3

Reading Comprehension

Time: 55 minutes

Now set your clock for 55 minutes.

Directions: In this section you will read several passages. Each one is followed by several questions about it. For questions 1–50, choose the one best answer—(A), (B), (C), or (D)—to each question. Then, on your answer sheet, find the number of the question and fill in the space that corresponds to the letter of the answer you have chosen.

Answer all questions following a passage on the basis of what is stated or implied in that passage.

Read the following passage.

The railroad was not the first institution to impose regularity on society or to draw attention to the importance of precise timekeeping. For as long as merchants have set out their wares at daybreak and communal festivities have been celebrated, people have been in rough
Line agreement with their neighbors as to the time of day. The value of this tradition is today
(5) more apparent than ever. Were it not for public acceptance of a single yardstick of time, social life would be unbearably chaotic; the massive daily transfers of goods, services, and information would proceed in fits and starts; the very fabric of modern society would begin to unravel.

Example I

Sample Answer

What is the main idea of the passage?

- (A) In modern society we must make more time for our neighbors.
- (B) The traditions of society are timeless.
- (C An accepted way of measuring time is essential for the smooth functioning of society.
- (D) Society judges people by the times at which they conduct certain activities.

The main idea of the passage is that societies need to agree about how time is to be measured in order to function smoothly. Therefore, you should choose (C).

Example II

Sample Answer
Ⓐ Ⓑ Ⓒ ●

In line 5, the phrase "this tradition" refers to

    (A) the practice of starting the business day at dawn
    (B) friendly relations between neighbors
    (C) the railroad's reliance on time schedules
    (D) people's agreement on the measurement of time

The phrase "this tradition" refers to the preceding clause, "people have been in rough agreement with their neighbors as to the time of day." Therefore, you should choose (D).

NOW BEGIN WORK ON THE QUESTIONS.

Questions 1–7

Hotels were among the earliest facilities that bound the United States together.
They were both creatures and creators of communities, as well as symptoms of the
frenetic quest for community. Even in the first part of the nineteenth century, Americans
Line were already forming the habit of gathering from all corners of the nation for both public
(5) and private, business and pleasure, purposes. Conventions were the new occasions, and
hotels were distinctively American facilities making conventions possible. The first
national convention of a major party to choose a candidate for president (that of the
National Republican Party, which met on December 12, 1831, and nominated Henry Clay
for president) was held in Baltimore, at a hotel that was then reputed to be the best in the
(10) country. The presence in Baltimore of Barnum's City Hotel, a six-story building with two
hundred apartments, helps explain why many other early national political conventions
were held there.

In the longer run, American hotels made other national conventions not only
possible but pleasant and convivial. The growing custom of regularly assembling from
(15) afar the representatives of all kinds of groups—not only for political conventions, but
also for commercial, professional, learned, and avocational ones—in turn supported
the multiplying hotels. By the mid-twentieth century, conventions accounted for over
a third of the yearly room occupancy of all hotels in the nation; about 18,000 different
conventions were held annually with a total attendance of about ten million persons.

(20) Nineteenth-century American hotelkeepers, who were no longer the genial,
deferential "hosts" of the eighteenth-century European inn, became leading citizens.
Holding a large stake in the community, they exercised power to make it prosper. As
owners or managers of the local "palace of the public," they were makers and shapers of
a principal community attraction. Travelers from abroad were mildly shocked by this high
(25) social position.

1. The word "bound" in line 1 is closest in meaning to

   (A) led
   (B) protected
   (C) tied
   (D) strengthened

2. The National Republican Party is mentioned in line 8 as an example of a group

   (A) from Baltimore
   (B) of learned people
   (C) owning a hotel
   (D) holding a convention

3. The word "assembling" in line 14 is closest in meaning to

   (A) announcing
   (B) motivating
   (C) gathering
   (D) contracting

4. The word "ones" in line 16 refers to

   (A) hotels
   (B) conventions
   (C) kinds
   (D) representatives

5. The word "it" in line 22 refers to

   (A) European inn
   (B) host
   (C) community
   (D) public

6. It can be inferred from the passage that early hotelkeepers in the United States were

   (A) active politicians
   (B) European immigrants
   (C) professional builders
   (D) influential citizens

7. Which of the following statements about early American hotels is NOT mentioned in the passage?

   (A) Travelers from abroad did not enjoy staying in them.
   (B) Conventions were held in them.
   (C) People used them for both business and pleasure.
   (D) They were important to the community.

Questions 8–15

    With Robert Laurent and William Zorach, direct carving enters into the story of modern sculpture in the United States. Direct carving—in which the sculptors themselves carve stone or wood with mallet and chisel—must be recognized as
Line something more than just a technique. Implicit in it is an aesthetic principle as well:
(5) that the medium has certain qualities of beauty and expressiveness with which sculptors must bring their own aesthetic sensibilities into harmony. For example, sometimes the shape or veining in a piece of stone or wood suggests, perhaps even dictates, not only the ultimate form, but even the subject matter.

    The technique of direct carving was a break with the nineteenth-century tradition in
(10) which the making of a clay model was considered the creative act and the work was then turned over to studio assistants to be cast in plaster or bronze or carved in marble. Neoclassical sculptors seldom held a mallet or chisel in their own hands, readily conceding that the assistants they employed were far better than they were at carving the finished marble.

(15)   With the turn-of-the-century Arts and Crafts movement and the discovery of nontraditional sources of inspiration, such as wooden African figures and masks, there arose a new urge for hands-on, personal execution of art and an interaction with the medium. Even as early as the 1880s and 1890s, nonconformist European artists were attempting direct carving. By the second decade of the twentieth century, Americans—Laurent
(20) and Zorach most notably—had adopted it as their primary means of working.

    Born in France, Robert Laurent (1890–1970) was a prodigy who received his education in the United States. In 1905 he was sent to Paris as an apprentice to an art dealer, and in the years that followed he witnessed the birth of Cubism, discovered primitive art, and learned the techniques of woodcarving from a frame maker.

(25)   Back in New York City by 1910, Laurent began carving pieces such as *The Priestess*, which reveals his fascination with African, pre-Columbian, and South Pacific art. Taking a walnut plank, the sculptor carved the expressive, stylized design. It is one of the earliest examples of direct carving in American sculpture. The plank's form dictated the rigidly frontal view and the low relief. Even its irregular shape must
(30) have appealed to Laurent as a break with a long-standing tradition that required a sculptor to work within a perfect rectangle or square.

8. The word "medium" in line 5 could be used to refer to

   (A) stone or wood
   (B) mallet and chisel
   (C) technique
   (D) principle

9. What is one of the fundamental principles of direct carving?

   (A) A sculptor must work with talented assistants.
   (B) The subject of a sculpture should be derived from classical stories.
   (C) The material is an important element in a sculpture.
   (D) Designing a sculpture is a more creative activity than carving it.

10. The word "dictates" in line 8 is closest in meaning to

    (A) reads aloud
    (B) determines
    (C) includes
    (D) records

11. How does direct carving differ from the nineteenth-century tradition of sculpture?

    (A) Sculptors are personally involved in the carving of a piece.
    (B) Sculptors find their inspiration in neoclassical sources.
    (C) Sculptors have replaced the mallet and chisel with other tools.
    (D) Sculptors receive more formal training.

12. The word "witnessed" in line 23 is closest in meaning to

    (A) influenced
    (B) studied
    (C) validated
    (D) observed

13. Where did Robert Laurent learn to carve?

    (A) New York
    (B) Africa
    (C) The South Pacific
    (D) Paris

14. The phase "a break with" in line 30 is closest in meaning to

    (A) a destruction of
    (B) a departure from
    (C) a collapse of
    (D) a solution to

15. The piece titled *The Priestess* has all of the following characteristics EXCEPT:

    (A) The design is stylized.
    (B) It is made of marble.
    (C) The carving is not deep.
    (D) It depicts the front of a person.

Questions 16–26

Birds that feed in flocks commonly retire together into roosts. The reasons for roosting communally are not always obvious, but there are some likely benefits. In winter especially, it is important for birds to keep warm at night and conserve precious food

Line reserves. One way to do this is to find a sheltered roost. Solitary roosters shelter in
(5) dense vegetation or enter a cavity—horned larks dig holes in the ground and ptarmigan burrow into snow banks—but the effect of sheltering is magnified by several birds huddling together in the roosts, as wrens, swifts, brown creepers, bluebirds, and anis do. Body contact reduces the surface area exposed to the cold air, so the birds keep each other warm. Two kinglets huddling together were found to
(10) reduce their heat losses by a quarter, and three together saved a third of their heat.

The second possible benefit of communal roosts is that they act as information centers. During the day, parties of birds will have spread out to forage over a very large area. When they return in the evening some will have fed well, but others may have found little to eat. Some investigators have observed that when the birds set out
(15) again next morning, those birds that did not feed well on the previous day appear to follow those that did. The behavior of common and lesser kestrels may illustrate different feeding behaviors of similar birds with different roosting habits. The common kestrel hunts vertebrate animals in a small, familiar hunting ground, whereas the very similar lesser kestrel feeds on insects over a large area. The common kestrel roosts and
(20) hunts alone, but the lesser kestrel roosts and hunts in flocks, possibly so that one bird can learn from others where to find insect swarms.

Finally, there is safety in numbers at communal roosts since there will always be a few birds awake at any given moment to give the alarm. But this increased protection is partially counteracted by the fact that mass roosts attract predators and are especially
(25) vulnerable if they are on the ground. Even those in trees can be attacked by birds of prey. The birds on the edge are at greatest risk since predators find it easier to catch small birds perching at the margins of the roost.

16. What does the passage mainly discuss?

    (A) How birds find and store food
    (B) How birds maintain body heat in the winter
    (C) Why birds need to establish territory
    (D) Why some species of birds nest together

17. The word "conserve" in line 3 is closest in meaning to

    (A) retain
    (B) watch
    (C) locate
    (D) share

18. Ptarmigan keep warm in the winter by

    (A) huddling together on the ground with other birds
    (B) building nests in trees
    (C) burrowing into dense patches of vegetation
    (D) digging tunnels into the snow

19. The word "magnified" in line 6 is closest in meaning to

    (A) caused
    (B) modified
    (C) intensified
    (D) combined

20. The author mentions kinglets in line 9 as an example of birds that

    (A) protect themselves by nesting in holes
    (B) nest with other species of birds
    (C) nest together for warmth
    (D) usually feed and nest in pairs

21. The word "forage" in line 12 is closest in meaning to

    (A) fly
    (B) assemble
    (C) feed
    (D) rest

22. Which of the following statements about lesser and common kestrels is true?

    (A) The lesser kestrel and the common kestrel have similar diets.
    (B) The lesser kestrel feeds sociably, but the common kestrel does not.
    (C) The common kestrel nests in larger flocks than does the lesser kestrel.
    (D) The common kestrel nests in trees; the lesser kestrel nests on the ground.

23. The word "counteracted' in line 24 is closest in meaning to

    (A) suggested
    (B) negated
    (C) measured
    (D) shielded

24. Which of the following is NOT mentioned in the passage as an advantage derived by birds that huddle together while sleeping?

    (A) Some members of the flock warn others of impending dangers.
    (B) Staying together provides a greater amount of heat for the whole flock.
    (C) Some birds in the flock function as information centers for others who are looking for food.
    (D) Several members of the flock care for the young.

25. Which of the following is a disadvantage of communal roosts that is mentioned in the passage?

    (A) Diseases easily spread among the birds.
    (B) Groups are more attractive to predators than individual birds are.
    (C) Food supplies are quickly depleted.
    (D) Some birds in the group will attack the others.

26. The word "they" in line 25 refers to

    (A) a few birds
    (B) mass roosts
    (C) predators
    (D) trees

SECTION 3 CONTINUES.
TURN THE PAGE AND READ THE NEXT PASSAGE.

Questions 27–38

Perhaps the most striking quality of satiric literature is its freshness, its originality of perspective. Satire rarely offers original ideas. Instead, it presents the familiar in a new form. Satirists do not offer the world new philosophies. What they do is look at

Line familiar conditions from a perspective that makes these conditions seem foolish,
(5) harmful, or affected. Satire jars us out of complacence into a pleasantly shocked realization that many of the values we unquestioningly accept are false. *Don Quixote* makes chivalry seem absurd; *Brave New World* ridicules the pretensions of science; *A Modest Proposal* dramatizes starvation by advocating cannibalism. None of these ideas is original. Chivalry was suspect before Cervantes, humanists objected to the claims of

(10) pure science before Aldous Huxley, and people were aware of famine before Swift. It was not the originality of the idea that made these satires popular. It was the manner of expression, the satiric method, that made them interesting and entertaining. Satires are read because they are aesthetically satisfying works of art, not because they are morally wholesome or ethically instructive. They are stimulating and refreshing because with

(15) commonsense briskness they brush away illusions and secondhand opinions. With spontaneous irreverence, satire rearranges perspectives, scrambles familiar objects into incongruous juxtaposition, and speaks in a personal idiom instead of abstract platitude.

Satire exists because there is need for it. It has lived because readers appreciate a refreshing stimulus, an irreverent reminder that they live in a world of platitudinous

(20) thinking, cheap moralizing, and foolish philosophy. Satire serves to prod people into an awareness of truth, though rarely to any action on behalf of truth. Satire tends to remind people that much of what they see, hear, and read in popular media is sanctimonious, sentimental, and only partially true. Life resembles in only a slight degree the popular image of it. Soldiers rarely hold the ideals that movies attribute to

(25) them, nor do ordinary citizens devote their lives to unselfish service of humanity. Intelligent people know these things but tend to forget them when they do not hear them expressed.

27. What does the passage mainly discuss?

    (A) Difficulties of writing satiric literature
    (B) Popular topics of satire
    (C) New philosophies emerging from satiric literature
    (D) Reasons for the popularity of satire

28. The word "realization" in line 6 is closest in meaning to

    (A) certainty
    (B) awareness
    (C) surprise
    (D) confusion

29. Why does the author mention *Don Quixote*, *Brave New World*, and *A Modest Proposal* in lines 6–8 ?

    (A) They are famous examples of satiric literature.
    (B) They present commonsense solutions to problems.
    (C) They are appropriate for readers of all ages.
    (D) They are books with similar stories.

30. The word "aesthetically" in line 13 is closest in meaning to

    (A) artistically
    (B) exceptionally
    (C) realistically
    (D) dependably

31. Which of the following can be found in satiric literature?

    (A) Newly emerging philosophies
    (B) Odd combinations of objects and ideas
    (C) Abstract discussion of morals and ethics
    (D) Wholesome characters who are unselfish

32. According to the passage, there is a need for satire because people need to be

    (A) informed about new scientific developments
    (B) exposed to original philosophies when they are formulated
    (C) reminded that popular ideas are often inaccurate
    (D) told how they can be of service to their communities

33. The word "refreshing" in line 19 is closest in meaning to

    (A) popular
    (B) ridiculous
    (C) meaningful
    (D) unusual

34. The word "they" in line 22 refers to

    (A) people
    (B) media
    (C) ideals
    (D) movies

35. The word "devote" in line 25 is closest in meaning to

    (A) distinguish
    (B) feel affection
    (C) prefer
    (D) dedicate

36. As a result of reading satiric literature, readers will be most likely to

    (A) teach themselves to write fiction
    (B) accept conventional points of view
    (C) become better informed about current affairs
    (D) reexamine their opinions and values

37. The various purposes of satire include all of the following EXCEPT

    (A) introducing readers to unfamiliar situations
    (B) brushing away illusions
    (C) reminding readers of the truth
    (D) exposing false values

38. Why does the author mention "service of humanity" in line 25 ?

    (A) People need to be reminded to take action.
    (B) Readers appreciate knowing about it.
    (C) It is an ideal that is rarely achieved.
    (D) Popular media often distort such stories.

SECTION 3 CONTINUES.
TURN THE PAGE AND READ THE NEXT PASSAGE.

Questions 39–50

Galaxies are the major building blocks of the universe. A galaxy is a giant family of many millions of stars, and it is held together by its own gravitational field. Most of the material in the universe is organized into galaxies of stars, together with gas and dust.

Line
(5)
There are three main types of galaxies: spiral, elliptical, and irregular. The Milky Way is a spiral galaxy: a flattish disc of stars with two spiral arms emerging from its central nucleus. About one-quarter of all galaxies have this shape. Spiral galaxies are well supplied with the interstellar gas in which new stars form; as the rotating spiral pattern sweeps around the galaxy, it compresses gas and dust, triggering the formation of bright young stars in its arms. The elliptical galaxies have a symmetrical, elliptical or
(10)
spheroidal shape with no obvious structure. Most of their member stars are very old, and since ellipticals are devoid of interstellar gas, no new stars are forming in them. The biggest and brightest galaxies in the universe are ellipticals with masses of about 1013 times that of the Sun; these giants may frequently be sources of strong radio emission, in which case they are called radio galaxies. About two-thirds of all galaxies
(15)
are elliptical. Irregular galaxies comprise about one-tenth of all galaxies, and they come in many subclasses.

Measurement in space is quite different from measurement on Earth. Some terrestrial distances can be expressed as intervals of time: the time to fly from one continent to another or the time it takes to drive to work, for example. By comparison,
(20)
with these familiar yardsticks, the distances to the galaxies are incomprehensibly large, but they too are made more manageable by using a time calibration, in this case, the distance that light travels in one year. On such a scale, the nearest giant spiral galaxy, the Andromeda galaxy, is two million light years away. The most distant luminous objects seen by telescopes are probably ten thousand million light years away. Their
(25)
light was already halfway here before the Earth even formed. The light from the nearby Virgo galaxy set out when reptiles still dominated the animal world.

39. The word "major" in line 1 is closest in meaning to

    (A) intense
    (B) principal
    (C) huge
    (D) unique

40. What does the second paragraph mainly discuss?

    (A) The Milky Way
    (B) Major categories of galaxies
    (C) How elliptical galaxies are formed
    (D) Differences between irregular and spiral galaxies

41. The word "which" in line 7 refers to

    (A) dust
    (B) gas
    (C) pattern
    (D) galaxy

42. According to the passage, new stars are formed in spiral galaxies due to

    (A) an explosion of gas
    (B) the compression of gas and dust
    (C) the combining of old stars
    (D) strong radio emissions

43. The word "symmetrical" in line 9 is closest in meaning to

    (A) proportionally balanced
    (B) commonly seen
    (C) typically large
    (D) steadily growing

44. The word "obvious" in line 10 is closest in meaning to

    (A) discovered
    (B) apparent
    (C) understood
    (D) simplistic

45. According to the passage, which of the following is NOT true of elliptical galaxies?

    (A) They are the largest galaxies.
    (B) They mostly contain old stars.
    (C) They contain a high amount of interstellar gas.
    (D) They have a spherical shape.

46. Which of the following characteristics of radio galaxies is mentioned in the passage?

    (A) They are a type of elliptical galaxy.
    (B) They are usually too small to be seen with a telescope.
    (C) They are closely related to irregular galaxies.
    (D) They are not as bright as spiral galaxies.

47. What percentage of galaxies is irregular?

    (A) 10%
    (B) 25%
    (C) 50%
    (D) 75%

48. The word "they" in line 21 refers to

    (A) intervals
    (B) yardsticks
    (C) distances
    (D) galaxies

49. Why does the author mention the Virgo galaxy and the Andromeda galaxy in the third paragraph?

    (A) To describe the effect that distance has on visibility
    (B) To compare the ages of two relatively young galaxies
    (C) To emphasize the vast distances of the galaxies from Earth
    (D) To explain why certain galaxies cannot be seen by a telescope

50. The word "dominated" in line 26 is closest in meaning to

    (A) threatened
    (B) replaced
    (C) were developing in
    (D) were prevalent in

THIS IS THE END OF THE READING COMPREHENSION SECTION.

IF YOU FINISH IN LESS THAN 55 MINUTES, CHECK YOUR WORK IN THIS SECTION ONLY.

DO NOT READ OR WORK ON ANY OTHER SECTION OF THE TEST.

WHEN YOU ARE READY TO CHECK YOUR ANSWERS, USE THE ANSWER KEY ON THE FOLLOWING PAGES TO DETERMINE WHICH QUESTIONS YOU ANSWERED CORRECTLY AND INCORRECTLY.

Answer Key

Section 1 Listening Comprehension		Section 2 Structure and Written Expression		Section 3 Reading Comprehension	
Question Number	Answer	Question Number	Answer	Question Number	Answer
1.	C	1.	A	1.	C
2.	B	2.	A	2.	D
3.	A	3.	B	3.	C
4.	A	4.	B	4.	B
5.	A	5.	B	5.	C
6.	A	6.	D	6.	D
7.	C	7.	D	7.	A
8.	A	8.	A	8.	A
9.	C	9.	C	9.	C
10.	B	10.	D	10.	B
11.	A	11.	C	11.	A
12.	B	12.	C	12.	D
13.	B	13.	D	13.	D
14.	A	14.	D	14.	B
15.	A	15.	A	15.	B
16.	B	16.	C	16.	D
17.	D	17.	B	17.	A
18.	D	18.	B	18.	D
19.	C	19.	A	19.	C
20.	B	20.	D	20.	C
21.	C	21.	C	21.	C
22.	D	22.	D	22.	B
23.	D	23.	D	23.	B
24.	C	24.	C	24.	D
25.	D	25.	A	25.	B
26.	C	26.	C	26.	B
27.	C	27.	D	27.	D
28.	A	28.	B	28.	B
29.	C	29.	D	29.	A
30.	D	30.	C	30.	A
31.	A	31.	A	31.	B
32.	B	32.	D	32.	C
33.	D	33.	A	33.	D
34.	B	34.	C	34.	A
35.	B	35.	B	35.	D
36.	D	36.	A	36.	D

Section 1 Listening Comprehension		Section 2 Structure and Written Expression		Section 3 Reading Comprehension	
Question Number	Answer	Question Number	Answer	Question Number	Answer
37.	C	37.	C	37.	A
38.	C	38.	B	38.	C
39.	B	39.	A	39.	B
40.	A	40.	C	40.	B
41.	A			41.	B
42.	C			42.	B
43.	D			43.	A
44.	C			44.	B
45.	B			45.	C
46.	A			46.	A
47.	D			47.	A
48.	B			48.	C
49.	C			49.	C
50.	B			50.	D

SCRIPT FOR SECTION 1—LISTENING COMPREHENSION

Part A

Questions 1–30

1. *Man:* Would you like to go to the movies with Lois and me on Friday?
   Woman: I wish I could, but I'm having dinner at my brother's.

   Narrator: What will the woman do on Friday?

2. *Man:* Need a hand with those boxes?
   Woman: That's OK, I can manage. They're empty.

   Narrator: What does the woman mean?

3. *Woman:* Do you want the windows open or closed?
   Man: I almost always prefer fresh air, if possible.

   Narrator: What does the man imply?

4. *Man:* Hello. This is Mark Smith. I'm calling to see if my blood test results are in.
   Woman: Dr. Miller just sent them to the lab last night, so the earliest they could be back is tomorrow.

   Narrator: What does the woman mean?

5. *Man:* I need to talk to someone who knows a lot about Portland. Someone said you lived there.
   Woman: Oh, but I was really young at the time.

   Narrator: What does the woman imply?

6. *Man:* Do you have to play that music so loud? I've got a test tomorrow!
   Woman: Sorry, I didn't realize you were studying.

   Narrator: What will the woman probably do?

7. *Man:* Pam, I don't understand the problem. You've known for months this report was due today.
   Woman: I know. But I'm afraid I need another few days. The data was harder to interpret than I thought it would be.

   Narrator: What does the woman mean?

8. *Woman:* So how are you getting along with Debbie's cat?
   Man: Well, she never comes when I call her, she spills her food, and she sheds all over the place. I can't wait till Debbie gets back.

   Narrator: What does the man imply?

9. **Man:** This crazy bus schedule has got me completely frustrated. I can't for the life of me figure out when my bus to Cleveland leaves.
Woman: Why don't you just go up to the ticket window and ask?

Narrator: What does the woman suggest the man do?

10. **Man:** I bought this fish to cook for my dinner tonight, but it doesn't look all that fresh to me now. Would you say it's still all right to eat?
Woman: Let's take a look. Oh, if I were you, I wouldn't even think of it.

Narrator: What does the woman mean?

11. **Man:** Would you like to go with me to the airport to pick up Frank?
Woman: I'd like to, but I have class till 2:00. And I know Frank's decided to take the early flight.

Narrator: What does the woman imply?

12. **Woman:** Did you catch our very own Professor Stiller on TV last night?
Man: I almost missed it! But my mother just happened to be watching at home and gave me a call.

Narrator: What does the man mean?

13. **Woman:** These summer days are getting to be more than I can take. It was even too hot to go to the pool yesterday.
Man: Hold on; according to the weather report we should have some relief by the end of the week.

Narrator: What does the man mean?

14. **Man:** My roommate and I have decided to do our own cooking next semester.
Woman: Then I hope you'll have a lighter schedule than this term.

Narrator: What problem does the woman think the man may have?

15. **Woman:** Come on, we're almost there. I'll race you to the top of the hill.
Man: I'm so out of shape, I might have to crawl the rest of the way.

Narrator: What can be inferred about the man?

16. **Man:** Yes, hello, this is Robert White calling. Could Dr. Jones see me on Tuesday morning instead of Thursday afternoon?
Woman: Tuesday morning? Let's see . . . is that the only other time you could come?

Narrator: What does the woman imply?

17. **Man:** I really need to make some extra money. I've practically spent my entire budget for the semester.
    Woman: You should check out the new cafeteria. I think there're a few openings left in the evening.

    Narrator: What does the woman suggest the man do?

18. **Man:** These long drives always wear me out. Instead of just stopping at a fast-food place, why don't we take some time out for a nice lunch?
    Woman: That's a great idea! It'll make the trip a bit longer, but at least we'll be refreshed when we get there.

    Narrator: What will the speakers probably do?

19. **Man:** This notice says that all the introductory psychology classes are closed.
    Woman: That can't be true! There're supposed to be thirteen sections of it this semester.

    Narrator: What does the woman mean?

20. **Woman:** Whoops! Did any of my coffee just spill on you?
    Man: Just a little, but it wasn't really hot.

    Narrator: What does the man imply?

21. **Woman:** Oh, my shirt sleeve. Must have gotten caught on that nail.
    Man: Here, let me take a look. Hmm . . . with a needle and thread, this can be mended—and look just like new.

    Narrator: What does the man mean?

22. **Woman:** I'm looking for a lightweight jacket . . . navy blue . . . medium . . .
    Man: Let's see. Have you checked the sales rack in the back? There were still a few there yesterday.

    Narrator: What does the man mean?

23. **Man:** I've figured it all out. It looks like it'll take us about six hours to drive from here to Chicago.
    Woman: It'd be more relaxing to take the train. But, I guess we should watch our expenses.

    Narrator: What does the woman imply?

24. **Man:** I've been working out at the gym since January . . . I'd been wanting to get in better shape.
    Woman: You look terrific! Seems like all your hard work has paid off.

    Narrator: What does the woman mean?

25. **Man:** This heat is unbearable. If only we'd gone to the beach instead.
    Woman: Why, with the museums and restaurants in Washington, I'd be happy here no matter what the weather.

    Narrator: What does the woman mean?

26. **Man:** I can't believe you stayed so calm last weekend when my Mom brought my little brother to visit. He practically wrecked the dorm lounge!
    Woman: Don't be so hard on him. He's only four.

    Narrator: What does the woman imply?

27. **Woman:** When's a good time to get together to discuss our history project?
    Man: Other than this Wednesday, one day's as good as the next.

    Narrator: What does the man mean?

28. **Man:** Congratulations! I heard your field hockey team is going to the mid-Atlantic championships!
    Woman: Yeah! Now we're all working hard to get ready for our game tomorrow.

    Narrator: What will the woman probably do this afternoon?

29. **Man:** On Saturday evenings, I usually meet some friends for dinner at a café near campus. Would you like to join us?
    Woman: I'm up to my ears in work, so I'll have to take a rain check.

    Narrator: What does the woman mean?

30. **Woman:** If you rub some soap on that drawer, it might stop sticking.
    Man: Well, maybe, but if I took out the paper that has fallen down in back, that would help, for sure.

    Narrator: What is the problem?

Part B

Questions 31–34

Narrator: Listen to a discussion about the Ice Age.

Man: Hey, Jane! What's so interesting?

Woman: What? Oh hi, Tom. I'm reading this fascinating article on the societies of the Ice Age during the Pleistocene [PLY-stuh-seen] period.

Man: The Ice Age? There weren't any societies then—there were just small groups of people living in caves, right?

Woman: That's what people used to think. But a new exhibit at the American Museum of Natural History shows that Ice Age people were surprisingly advanced.

Man: Oh, really? In what ways?

Woman: Well, Ice Age people were the inventors of language, art, and music as we know it. And they didn't live in caves; they built their own shelters.

Man: What did they use to build them? The cold weather would have killed off most of the trees, so they couldn't have used wood.

Woman: In some of the warmer climates they did build houses of wood. In other places they used animal bones and skins or lived in natural stone shelters.

Man: How did they stay warm? Animal-skin walls don't sound very sturdy.

Woman: Well, it says here that in the early Ice Age they often faced their homes toward the south to take advantage of the sun—a primitive sort of solar heating.

Man: Hey, that's pretty smart.

Woman: Then people in the late Ice Age even insulated their homes by putting heated cobblestones on the floor.

Man: I guess I spoke too soon. Can I read that magazine article after you're done? I think I'm gonna try to impress my anthropology teacher with my amazing knowledge of Ice Age civilization.

Woman: [laughing] What a show-off!

31. *Narrator:* What did the man think about people of the Ice Age?

32. *Narrator:* What does the woman say about the use of wood during the Ice Age?

33. *Narrator:* How did people in the early Ice Age keep warm?

34. *Narrator:* What does the man want the woman to do?

Narrator: Listen to a conversation between two students.

Man: I really appreciate your filling me in on yesterday's lecture.

Woman: No problem, I thought you might want to go over it together. And, anyway, it helps me review. Hope you're feeling better now.

Man: I am. Thanks. So, you said she talked about squid? Sounds a little strange.

Woman: Well, actually, it was about the evolution of sea life—a continuation from last week. The octopus and the squid descended from earlier creatures with shells. They survived by shedding their shells—somewhere between 200 and 500 million years ago.

Man: That's a pretty long span of time.

Woman: I know. That's what she said, though. To be precise: "Exactly when they emerged is uncertain, and why is still unexplained."

Man: Some squid are really huge. Can you imagine something that big if it still had a shell?

Woman: Actually, it's because they lost their shells that they could evolve to a bigger size.

Man: Makes sense. I've read about fishermen who caught squid that weighed over a ton. Did she talk about how that happens?

Woman: Not really. But she did mention some unusual cases. In 1933 in New Zealand, they caught a giant squid . . . let's see here . . . it was 20 meters long. Its eyes were almost 46 centimeters across. Can you imagine?

Man: Reminds me of all those stories of sea monsters.

Woman: Professor Simpson thinks there are probably even larger ones that haven't been found because squid are intelligent and fast—so they can easily get away from humans. Maybe some of those monster stories are true.

35. *Narrator:* What topic are the man and woman discussing?

36. *Narrator:* Why does the man need to talk to the woman about the class?

37. *Narrator:* According to the woman, what happened 200 to 500 million years ago?

38. *Narrator:* What does the woman imply about sea monsters?

Part C

Narrator: Listen to a professor talk to new students about an experiment in child development.

Woman: In our lab today, we'll be testing the hypothesis that babies can count as early as five months of age. The six babies here are all less than six months old. You'll be watching them on closed-circuit TV and measuring their responses.

The experiment is based on the well-established observation that babies stare longer if they don't see what they expect to see. First, we're going to let two dolls move slowly in front of the babies. The babies will see the two dolls disappear behind a screen. Your job is to record, in seconds, how long the babies stare at the dolls when the screen is removed.

In the next stage, two dolls will again move in front of the babies and disappear. But then a third doll will follow. When the screen is removed, the babies will only see two dolls. If we're right, the babies will now stare longer because they expect three dolls but only see two.

It seems remarkable to think that such young children can count. My own research has convinced me that they have this ability from birth. But whether they do or not, perhaps we should raise another question—should we take advantage of this ability by teaching children mathematics at such a young age? They have great untapped potential, but is it good for parents to pressure young children?

39. *Narrator:* What is the experiment designed to demonstrate?

40. *Narrator:* Which of the babies' reactions would be significant for the purposes of the experiment?

41. *Narrator:* How does the professor explain the babies' behavior?

42. *Narrator:* What implication of her research is the professor concerned about?

Narrator: Listen to part of a lecture in a geology class.

Man: I'm glad you brought up the question of our investigations into the makeup of Earth's interior. In fact—since this is the topic of your reading assignment for next time—let me spend these last few minutes of class talking about it. There were several important discoveries that helped geologists develop a more accurate picture of Earth's interior.

The first key discovery had to do with seismic waves—remember they are the vibrations caused by earthquakes. Well, scientists found that they traveled thousands of miles through Earth's interior. This finding enabled geologists to study the inner parts of the Earth. You see, these studies revealed that these vibrations were of two types: compression—or P—waves and shear—or S—waves. And researchers found that P waves travel through both liquids and solids, while S waves travel only through solid matter.

In 1906 a British geologist discovered that P waves slowed down at a certain depth but kept traveling deeper. On the other hand, S waves either disappeared or were reflected back, so he concluded that the depth marked the boundary between a solid mantle and a liquid core. Three years later another boundary was discovered—that between the mantle and Earth's crust.

There's still a lot to be learned about Earth. For instance, geologists know that the core is hot. Evidence of this is the molten lava that flows out of volcanoes. But we're still not sure what the source of the heat is.

43. *Narrator:* What is the purpose of the talk?

44. *Narrator:* What important discovery about seismic waves does the instructor mention?

45. *Narrator:* What did the study of seismic vibrations help geologists learn more about?

46. *Narrator:* What did P and S waves help scientists discover about the layers of Earth?

Narrator: Listen to part of a talk in an art history class.

Woman: You may remember that a few weeks ago we discussed the question of what photography is. Is it art, or is it a method of reproducing images? Do photographs belong in museums or just in our homes? Today I want to talk about a person who tried to make his professional life an answer to such questions.

Alfred Stieglitz went from the United States to Germany to study engineering. While he was there, he became interested in photography and began to experiment with his camera. He took pictures under conditions that most photographers considered too difficult—he took them at night, in the rain, and of people and objects reflected in windows. When he returned to the United States, he continued these revolutionary efforts. Stieglitz was the first person to photograph skyscrapers, clouds, and views from an airplane.

What Stieglitz was trying to do in these photographs was what he tried to do throughout his life: make photography an art. He felt that photography could be just as good a form of self-expression as painting or drawing. For Stieglitz, his camera was his brush. While many photographers of the late 1800s and early 1900s thought of their work as a reproduction of identical images, Stieglitz saw his as a creative art form. He understood the power of the camera to capture the moment. In fact, he never retouched his prints or made copies of them. If he were in this classroom today, I'm sure he'd say, "Well, painters don't normally make extra copies of their paintings, do they?"

47. *Narrator:* What is the professor mainly discussing?

48. *Narrator:* What question had the professor raised in a previous class?

49. *Narrator:* What does the professor imply about the photographs Stieglitz took at night?

50. *Narrator:* Why did Stieglitz choose to not make copies of the photographs?

CHAPTER 7

Frequently Asked Questions

What is the *TOEFL ITP* test?

The *TOEFL ITP* test offers colleges and universities, English-language programs, and other organizations the opportunity to administer a convenient and reliable English-language assessment. The test measures English proficiency at intermediate to advanced levels.

The test uses academic content to evaluate your skills in three areas:

- Listening Comprehension
- Structure and Written Expression
- Reading Comprehension

Who uses the *TOEFL ITP* test?

Over 2,500 institutions in 47 countries administer 600,000 *TOEFL ITP* tests annually.

- Colleges and universities
- Secondary schools
- English-language programs
- Governments
- Agencies

How is the *TOEFL ITP* test used by my institution?

There are many ways that your institution can use the *TOEFL ITP* test.

- **Placement** in intensive English-language programs requiring academic English proficiency at a college or graduate level
- **Evaluation of progress** in English-language programs stressing academic English proficiency
- **Exit** from English-language programs by demonstrating proficiency in English listening and reading

- **Admission to short-term, non-degree programs in English-speaking countries** where the sending and receiving institutions agree to use *TOEFL ITP* scores

- **Admission to undergraduate and graduate degree programs in non-English speaking countries** where English is not the dominant form of instruction

- **Admission to and placement in collaborative international degree programs** where English-language training will be a feature of the program

- **Qualification for scholarship programs**, as contributing documentation of academic English proficiency

What skills does the *TOEFL ITP* test measure?

The *TOEFL ITP* test has three sections. Each section measures a different skill.

- **Listening Comprehension** measures the ability to understand spoken English as it is used in colleges and universities.

- **Structure and Written Expression** measures recognition of selected structural and grammatical points in standard written English.

- **Reading Comprehension** measures the ability to read and understand academic reading material written in English.

What is the format of the test?

TOEFL ITP tests are paper-based, multiple-choice tests. You answer questions by filling out an answer sheet. The test consists of three sections: Listening Comprehension, Structure and Written Expression, and Reading Comprehension.

How is the *TOEFL ITP* test administered?

The test is administered by your institution. Institutions set the test date and determine who will be tested. Students do not have to register individually with ETS to take the test.

How are the tests scored?

The tests are scored either locally or by ETS. Score reports are usually available within seven days. Each section is scored separately. You will receive a score report to help you determine which skills you need to improve, so you can tailor your English-language studies to your individual needs.